IN DANGER

IN DANGER

A Pasolini Anthology

Edited, with an introduction
by Jack Hirschman

City Lights Books
San Francisco, California

Cover photo by Angelo Novi
Cover and interior design by Linda Ronan

 City Lights would like to thank Amelia Carpenito Antonucci,
Valeria Rumori, and Manilo Gullotta of the Istituto Italiano di
Cultura for their generous support of this book.

Library of Congress Cataloging-in-Publication Data
Pasolini, Pier Paolo, 1922–1975.
  [Selections. English. 2010]
  In danger : a Pasolini anthology / edited, with an introduction by Jack
Hirschman.
     p. cm.
  A translated collection of Pasolini's prose, poetry, essays, reviews of books,
etc., including his well-known "I Know" litany.
  ISBN 978-0-87286-507-5
  1. Pasolini, Pier Paolo, 1922–1975—Translations into English. I. Hirschman,
Jack, 1933– II. Title.

  PQ4835.A48A2 2010
  851'.914—dc22

                              2010013386

Mixed Sources
Product group from well-managed
forests and other controlled sources
www.fsc.org Cert no. SW-COC-002283
© 1996 Forest Stewardship Council

Visit our website: www.citylights.com

City Lights Books are published at the City Lights Bookstore,
261 Columbus Avenue, San Francisco, CA 94133

CONTENTS

INTRODUCTION

When Lawrence Ferlinghetti asked me if I would like to put to-
gether as editor and participating translator an anthology of the
works of Pier Paolo Pasolini, I was both delighted and honored.
Over the past dozen or more years, no Western poet's work has
interested me more than has Pasolini's. In the mid-Nineties
I wrote a rather long "Arcane" on the meaning of his life, his
poetry, and his assassination; and about a decade later, for the
2004 American presidential election, I composed another "Ar-
cane" using the murder of Pasolini and the resurrection of his
voice to mount an attack on the war-dogs in Washington. Both
those works, to one degree or other, were also inspired by the
wonderful translations of Pasolini's *Roman Poems* by Lawrence
Ferlinghetti and Francesca Valente, published by City Lights in
1986 (and again in 2006), one of the very best books that the
press has ever published.

Over the past 20 years, many of Pasolini's poems have ap-
peared in translated collections, and a dozen years ago the Cas-
tro Theater in San Francisco dedicated two weeks to showing
virtually all of the many films he created, because Pasolini is
primarily known to the world of cinema aficionados and the
general intelligentsia as a "poet" in the art of movie-making.
Interestingly enough, however, the dynamism and profound
meaning of his written ideas—as they relate to the times we live
in—are not as well known to an American readership. This an-
thology hopes, in a small way (because the body of his prose
and theoretical writing is almost as immense as the body of his
poetry), to help with a deeper understanding of his ideas, and
of their importance.

Pasolini was a creative dynamo in the 53 years of his life and, had he not been assassinated in 1975, I have no doubt that he would have continued writing, with the lucid integrity and passions that are at the heart of his work, to this very day (*magari!*). He embodies an extraordinary fusion of creativity: a poet in his depths, an intellectual of a rare literary and political brilliance and polemical insight, a filmmaker who helped revolutionize that form in Italy and throughout the world, a playwright of great power, and a formidable painter as well.

Pasolini was 21 when the fascist regime fell in Italy. After the war, he entered the Italian Communist Party in the small town of San Giovanni, near the town of Casarsa in the northeastern area of Italy known as Friuli, where he had been raised. In fact he soon became the head of the local chapter and, in the Pasolini Museum, in the very house where he lived, I've seen a large poster written in the Friulian language with child-like printed letters, which Pasolini composed as a call to peasants and workers. Pasolini was however expelled from the Party after a short time. A homosexual, he was discovered in an assignation with a couple of other young men. The times could hardly bear that; the Party also could not. He was forced to flee Casarsa for Rome.

But he remained a communist till his dying breath. And, as an "outsider" within the revolutionary turmoil and struggle in Italy after the war, studying and being intellectually inspired by the writings of Antonio Gramsci, the founder of the Italian Communist Party who died in Mussolini's prison, Pasolini developed not simply as a poet but as the sounder of alarm with respect to the age of consumerism, which he predicted with prophetic accuracy would contaminate the working class with middle-class values, and create an endemic hedonism and pornographic banality that, along with the tragedy of drugs, would mask a fascism much more difficult to dispense with than the fascism of the Thirties and Forties.

Had Pasolini remained in the orthodoxy of the PCI,[1] I doubt that he would have arrived at such insights. In effect, as a poet, he developed into a provocateur and prophet—the two elements (provocation and prophecy) that are the basis of all his writings, whether poetry or prose. His thrust was toward independent insight while at the same time defending to the core the plight of the poor and marginalized—in Italy as well as the Third World countries he visited. And even when some of the positions he takes seem contradictory, or his views of this or that poet or writer seem myopic or "off the wall" (as in his takes on Pablo Neruda or Charles Olson, for example), there is hardly a paragraph of prose or a stanza of poetry that doesn't contain Pasolini's uniquely provocative and prophetic modernity. We who are living in the technologically-driven stage of a neo-capitalism that is both rapacious in the extreme and crumbling from within, and who are witnessing a globally new class of poor, new abolitionists stirring for the battle against worldwide economic slavery, will be inspired by Pasolini's lucid insights and feelings about both personal and political life, whether or not we agree with them.

This anthology is in five sections. Its title comes from the last two words of an interview he gave Furio Colombo on November 1, 1975, a few hours before he was brutally murdered.

The texts are presented chronologically in each section. The first section is made up of some striking pieces of his prose, including the opening "Civil War," which concerns Pasolini's visit to New York in 1966. His insights into American revolutionary

---

1. Italian Communist Party.

life and struggle—not merely in the sixties but valid even to-day—urged me to open the book with this text

The second section is a selection of his poems, from 1941 to 1963, two of them in the Friulian language (in which Pasolini also wrote throughout his life), and many which have not appeared before in the American language.

The third section is of literary essays and reviews of books written in the last three years of his life. Published in newspapers and literary magazines, they are presented to show that, in every literary form, Pasolini kept up an intense sociopolitical awareness and engagement with revolutionary struggle. These particular essays were chosen to reflect the wide range of subjects that obsessed him, including: consumerism, fascism, war, sex, violence, and, of course, good (or bad) writing.

The fourth section is another selection of poems, from 1964 to 1971.

The final section consists of two texts: his well-known "I Know" litany (which text some say was one of the reasons he was assassinated) and the interview Pasolini gave on the last day of his life.

This book would not have been possible without a brilliant array of translators. They include Lucia Gazzino, a poet of Udine, Italy, who writes in both Italian and Friulian and who translated Pasolini's Friulian poems; Pasquale Verdicchio, a poet in San Diego who's not only translated Pasolini in the past but also written a suite of poems dedicated to him; Giada Diano, who's from Reggio Calabria and is writing a book on Lawrence Ferlinghetti's European experiences; Flavio Rizzo, a filmmaker who's documented Pasolini on the screen and teaches comparative literature at Queens College in New York; and Veruska Cantelli, likewise a teacher of comparative literature at Queens

College, who's also a modern dancer. Also from New York, the poet Norman MacAfee, who is renowned for his translations of Pasolini's poems, has contributed the translation of "Victory" that he made with the Italian documentary filmmaker Luciano Martinengo. From San Francisco, the musician-singer Jonathan Richman, working with Jacopo Benci, has translated a number of pieces; Susanna Bonetti, a librarian at the Erik Erikson Psychoanalytical Library, has contributed the opening work; and I myself round out the team of translators. My thanks to all of them for their contributions to this anthology.

Sometimes, almost exclusively in Pasolini's prose essays, I've changed a colon to a comma, as Pier Paolo often wrote his sentences using colons rather than commas between clauses, as explanatory extensions. My changes are simply to actualize a more lucid experience for a readership not used to Pasolini's unorthodox manner of punctuation.

My especial thanks to Lawrence Ferlinghetti, who's provided many helpful editorial suggestions on the texts; to Graziella Chiarcossi of the Pasolini Estate in Italy for her help regarding the chronology of the works; to Giada Diano for her thorough work in providing key footnote information; to Amelia Carpenito Antonucci, Director of the Italian Cultural Institute of San Francisco, for her invaluable work in securing the cover photo of Pasolini; and to Garrett Caples, poet and editor with City Lights, who has also overseen the publication of this book.

Some of these translations have appeared in *City Lights Review*, *Left Curve*, *Brick*, *Partisans* (Deliriodendron Press), and the Parenthesis Writing Series. My thanks to their respective editors.

—Jack Hirschman, San Francisco 2009

PROVOCATIONS

CIVIL WAR

The observations on life and political struggle in the United States that I've synthesized and cited are from American authors of the New Left and particularly two ideologues of SNCC (Student Nonviolent Coordinating Committee), Tom Hayden and Jimmy Garrett. Hayden's observations are to the point that communist collectivization would not necessarily (historically) lead the worker to a complete participation in power, namely in decisions with respect to his own destiny; that the contrary is perhaps true, that is, the creation of an "anti-community," in which the worker would arrive at the exasperated democratic consciousness of duty toward human rights in complete participation, can lead as a consequence to a collectivization of goods. Jimmy Garrett makes the observation that the communist is a "hollow man." I quote: "Friend, communists are empty, hollow men. They have the same stale ideas, the same bureaucracy. . . . When he mixes with us, a 'commie' dies and a person develops."

These observations are not mine, but in a way I've adopted them.

In Czechoslovakia, Hungary, and Romania, I lived among intellectuals, and it was through their worries and stress that I felt the worries and stress of their countries, the cause of which can be sketchily and summarily indicated by the fact that "the revolution did not continue"—that is, the State did not decentralize, did not disappear, and the workers in the factories are not really participating in and responsible for political power. Instead they are dominated—who doesn't by now know it and admit it?—by a bureaucracy that is revolutionary in name only, and that naturally calls petty-bourgeois revolutionists those who still believe that revolution should continue.

It's very interesting, and it fires one's enthusiasm, to see that in America there are non-Marxist ideologues who understand this in democratic terms—but of an extremist democracy, exasperated and quasi-mystical and yet, in its sphere, revolutionary (the creation of an "anti-community" within the heart of the American community). SNCC, SDS, and many other movements that chaotically comprise the New American Left are reminders to me of Resistance times here in Italy.

In America, even though my visit was brief, I spent many hours in an underground atmosphere of struggle, revolutionary urgency, and hope that belongs to the Europe of 1944 and 1945. In Europe everything is finished; in America I have the impression that everything is going to begin. I don't mean to say that there's civil war in America, nor even something like it, and I don't want to predict such; nevertheless, one lives there as if one were on the eve of great things. Those who belong to the New Left (which doesn't exist, it's just an idea, an ideal) recognize each other at a glance, and there is immediately born between them the kind of love that bonded the partisans. There are the fallen heroes—Andrew, James, and Mickey, and many others— and the big motions, the huge strides of an immense popular movement concentrated on the problem of the emancipation of the Blacks, and now on the Vietnam War.

Who hasn't seen a pacifist and nonviolent demonstration in New York is lacking in a great human experience comparable only to the great days of hope of the Forties.

One night in Harlem I shook hands (though they were suspicious because I was white) with a group of young Blacks who were wearing the symbol of the panther on their sweaters—an extremist movement preparing for armed struggle.

One afternoon in the Village I saw a small group of neonazis demonstrating for the Vietnam War; nearby, two old men and a girl who was playing guitar, taken as if by a strange and gentle ecstasy, were singing the pacifist songs of the Village, including those of the beatnik Left, of the drug addicts.

I went with a Black union official to the headquarters of his movement, a small movement that in Harlem has only a few hundred subscribers, and which fights against Black unemployment; went with him to one of his comrades' home, a bricklayer who had gotten sick on the job and who met us stretched out on his humble bed with a friendly complicitous smile so full of that forgotten partisan love of ours.

I went to a middle-class flat in the most squalid part of the Village and heard the hysterical laughter and aberrant bitterness of an intellectual married to a Black man, who blathered resentment against the old American communism and against the drugged Left, as if her rage and burning delusions should immediately be responded to in her world, and suddenly become "action."

I've lived a situation altogether alive with discontent and exultation, with desperation and hope, in total protest against the establishment. I don't know how all this will end, or if it will end at all, but the fact remains that thousands of students (almost the percentile of partisans relative to the Italian population in the Forties) come from the North and go into the "Black Belt" to fight alongside Blacks with a violent and almost mystical democratic consciousness that "doesn't manipulate them" or in any way coerce them, even to softness, or make them pretend (and they're almost neurotic about this) to even the shadow of any form of "leadership"; and what is more important, with the consciousness that the Blacks' problem, formally solved with the recognition of their civil rights, begins then—that is, as a social, not an ideal problem.

There is still much to add: protest, pure and simple confrontation, the revolt against consumerism. I intend to speak of the phenomenon of the beatniks, which has been set up here in terms of pure curiosity, without need of underlining it with irony. Communists, in Italy at least, so far as I know, prefer to be silent on this subject, or just condemn it, an approach with which old Italian moralism and provincialism find an obscure identification. In reality, in the large American cities, the alcoholic, the drug addict, whoever refuses being integrated into the secure work-market, enacts more than a series of old and codified anarchist acts: he lives a tragedy.

And since he alone knows how to live it and not judge it, he dies of it.

The thousands of drug addicts are actually no more or less martyrs than are those killed by the white racists of the South. They have the same purity and are likewise beyond the miserable human calculations of those who accept the "quality of life" offered by established society.

It's true. Everything I saw or believed I'd see in New York stands out against a dark background—as inconceivable as it is inadmissible for us—that is, against everyday American life, the life of self-preservation that proceeds in a silence that's more intense than even the "screams" that come from the Left. In this silent background, neutral and terrible, phenomena happen that are of real collective craziness, in a codified hateful way that's difficult to describe. It is racist hatred—that is, nothing less than the exterior aspect of the deep aberration of every conservatism and every fascism. It is a hatred that doesn't have any reason to exist. As a matter of fact it doesn't exist. Whoever's affected by it believes he feels it; in reality he can't feel it. How and why could a poor white hate a Black? Yet it's the poor whites of the whole South who in practice live off this hate. It is born from the false idea of the self and therefore of reality; and it is thus false itself, a sentiment completely alienated and unrecognizable. From this form of life the ultimate and most tragic result is the unvindicated murder of Kennedy, a case of that civil war that doesn't explode but nonetheless is fought out in the souls of Americans.

Speaking always and only of neo-capitalism and the technological revolution with respect to America seems to me partial and sectarian. It seems absurd, but the problem of poverty and underdevelopment acquires a strange and violent meaning with respect to America. Indeed, it's clear to everybody that these are the times in which the rural world of the globe—the Third World—is confronting history (with one foot in prehistory), and the scandal is that, despite the great episodes of the Algerian and Cuban revolts, the core of the struggle for the Third World revolution is really America. The Black problem, linked in a very twisted yet inextricable way with that of the poor whites (in huge numbers, much more than what we think), is a Third World problem. And if this is a scandal for the work-consciousness of the European communist parties, it is even more so for American capitalistic consciousness, which believes itself to be objectively on the clear path of technical progress and economic wealth. So the Black problem will never be sufficiently considered because, I repeat, it is connected in a crazy and contradictory way with the problem of the poor or once-poor whites. Indeed, two or three generations have not been enough to completely transform the psychology of the enormous masses of immigrants. They (I saw it for sure in the Italian district) first of all keep an adoring disposition toward the country that took them in and, now that they are citizens, toward its institutions. They are still sons, sons too obedient or too desperate. Secondly, they've carried with them—preserved inside themselves—the principal characteristic of peasants of underdeveloped areas—in some way prehistoric—which DeMartino[1] defines as the "fear of losing heritage." These are the fundamentals of popular fascist racism.

There'll never be enough said about the differences among Americans because of their diverse poor origins.

Perhaps that's why they so desperately want to be equal, one with another, and if they found their anti-communism on the premise that communism would bring about an equalization of individuals, it's because they desperately want above all to be equalized. In order to forget their origins, diverse and inferior, which differentiate them as signs. Every American has an indelible mark printed on his face. The image of an Italian or of a Frenchman or an Englishman or an average German is conceivable and can be represented. The image of the standard American is absolutely inconceivable and unrepresentable. This is the thing that most surprised me in America. One always talks of an "average American," and then this "average American" doesn't

---

1. Ernesto DeMartino, 1908–1965, Italian philosopher and anthropologist.

exist! How to sum up in a single "type" all the extraordinary types that are walking around in Manhattan? How to sum up in a single face the nervous Anglo-Saxon face, the crazy one of the Irishman, the sad one of the Italian, the pale one of the Greek, the wild one of the Puerto Rican, the neurotic German one, the funny one of the Chinese, the adorable one of the Black. . . ?

It's therefore the "fear of losing heritage" and the snobbery of new citizenship that prevents the American—the strange, precise mixture of lumpen proletarian and bourgeois deeply and honestly closed in its own middle-class loyalty—from reflecting on the idea that he has of himself, an idea that remains false in any environment alienating through total industrialization.

Indeed I tried asking those Americans I could if they knew what racism is (a question that particularly implies a reflection on the idea of the self). Nobody knew how to answer. Excepting a few young independent filmmakers who, knowing Europe with love, have some idea of Marxism, all the others resorted to incredibly ingenuous ontologies. (There were only some correct psychoanalytic explanations that touched, however, only one side of the problem, or better, the human condition through which the problem gets started.)

In conclusion, the most violent, dramatic, and defining note of the "quality of American life" is a negative characteristic: the lack of class-consciousness, the immediate effect of the false idea of the individual self, admitted by concession or by grace to the circle of petty-bourgeois privilege of industrial wealth and governmental power.

But there are strong contradictions in this (I'm certainly not the first to point this out): for instance, the overflowing strength of the unionism that comes through incredibly efficient and enormous strikes where it's hard to understand how a solid class-consciousness couldn't take place, while it's clear to us that such well-organized, such strongly united strikes don't mean anything else but the vindication of the exploited against the exploiters.

The extraordinary originality (for a European like me) is that the class-consciousness, rather, crops up in Americans in situations that are all new, and scandalous for Marxism.

Class-consciousness, to get into the head of an American, needs a long, twisting road, an immensely complex operation: it needs the mediation of idealism, let's say the bourgeois or petty-bourgeois variety, which for every American gives meaning to his entire life and which he absolutely cannot disregard. There they call it spiritualism. But both idealism in our interpretation and spiritualism in theirs are two ambiguous and incorrect words. Better, perhaps, it's about the moralism (Anglo-Saxon in origin and naively adopted by the other Americans) that rules and shapes the facts of life, and that, in literature for instance—even the popular kind—is exactly the opposite of realism. Americans always need to idealize in the arts (especially at the level of average taste; for instance, the "illustrative" representation of their lives and their cities in their popular movies are forms of an immediate need to idealize).

So instead of strikes or other forms of struggle, the consciousness of their own social reality turns out in pacifist and nonviolent demonstrations dominated precisely by an intelligent spiritualism, which is, at least for me, a splendid fact objectively, for which reason I fell in love with America. It's the vision of the world of people arrived, through ways we consider wrong—but which historically are what they are, that is, correct—at the maturation of the idea of self as a simple citizen (perhaps like Athenians or Romans?), the possessor of an honest and deep notion of democracy (driven to almost mystic forms, revolutionary ones in some of the representatives of SNCC and SDS). Indeed, to arrive at a consciousness not merely formally democratic of self and society, the truly free American has had need of passing through the calvary of the Blacks (and now through the calvary of Vietnam) and sharing it. Today, after some years, some months, that is, since the formal recognition of the civil rights of Blacks, one has begun to understand that the Black issue is fundamental, and that it is a social issue and not an issue merely of democratic spiritualism and the civil code.

The immense void that opens like an abyss in individual Americans and in the whole of American society—that is, the lack of Marxist culture—as any void, violently claims to be filled. It is filled by that spiritualism that, as I've said, being at first revolutionary democratic radicalism, is now going through a new social consciousness that, not explicitly accepting Marxism, presents itself as total confrontation and anarchist desperation.

It's from this and not anything else that the Other America is born. It's upon this and not anything else that the premises of a possible Third Party are built, about which one talks with great and ingenuous caution, as if it were shockingly blasphemous, with hope or hostility. For instance, in two or three cities where (thanks to the student movement) an embryonic form of this party ran in the elections, it turned out that the party not only was defeated but also caused the defeat of the moderates, to the benefit of the racists.

Now, I live in a society just emerging from poverty and superstition, clinging to the little wealth it achieved as if this were a stable condition, and this society is carrying on this new historical path a common sense that served well on the farms for the herds or for the craftsmen's shops but that today manifests itself as stupid, nasty, and cowardly in our present world. An irredeemable society, irrecoverably bourgeois, without revolutionary or even liberal traditions. The world of culture—in which I live because of a literary vocation that every day proves itself more estranged from such a society and world—is the place delegated to stupidity, cowardice, and pettiness. I cannot accept anything of the world I live in, not only the apparatus of the central state—bureaucracy, judicial system, the army, the schools, and the rest of it—but also not even its learned minorities. In this particular instance I'm absolutely alien to the momentum of the current culture. I'm deaf to the purely verbal transgressions of the established institutions, which say nothing about who's behind them, and I'm deaf to the purist and neo-literary revanchism. Let's just say that I was left alone to turn yellow with myself and my revulsion for talking about engagement or detachment. So I could not not fall in love with American culture, having glimpsed within it a literary reason full of originality: a new Resistance that I must insist, however, lacks all that renaissance spirit, that classicism which—seen from today—impoverishes European Resistance a bit (whose hopes were otherwise contained in the Marxist perspectives of those years, which then revealed themselves as narrow and conventional).

What is required of a "not integrated" American man of letters is everything itself, a total sincerity. Since the old days of Machado[2] I have not given so fraternal a reading as I did with Ginsberg. And wasn't it marvelous: Kerouac's sloshing journey through Italy that provoked the irony, boredom, and disapproval of the stupid men of letters and vile Italian journalists? The American intellectuals of the New Left (because where it's in

---

2. Antonio Machado, Spanish poet whose work influenced Pasolini.

struggle there's always a guitar and someone singing) seem to be doing what a line of an innocent song of the Black resistance says: "You gotta throw your body into the fight." Here is the new motto of real, not annoyingly moralistic, commitment. Throw your body into the fight. . . . Who among writers in Italy, in Europe, is pulled by such desperate forces of contention? Who feels this necessity *to oppose* as an original necessity, believing that it is new in history, absolutely meaningful, and replete with both with death and the future?

1966. Translated by Susanna Bonetti

PIER PAOLO PASOLINI
INTERVIEWS EZRA POUND

PASOLINI "Oh let an old man rest."[1]

That's how this Canto ends. I well know, Pound, that I'm here to disturb your rest. But first, I must show you how I feel on meeting you. I'll read something you wrote. Do you remember one of your "Lustra" poems addressed to Walt Whitman? It says: "I make a pact with you, Walt Whitman—I have detested you long enough. I come to you as a grown child who has had a pig-headed father; I am old enough now to make friends. It was you that broke the new wood, now is a time for carving. We have one sap and one root—Let there be commerce between us."[2]

I could read this poem, changing only two little details: your name and one other thing. I'd read it thus: "I make a pact with you *Ezra Pound*—I have detested you long enough. I come to you as a grown child who has had a pig-headed father; I am old enough now to make friends. It was you who began carving, now is the time to break the new wood. We have one sap and one root—let there be commerce between us."

POUND Fine, friends then: *pax tibi, pax mundi.*

PASOLINI There's another point I'd like to make. I'd like to ask you brutally how you feel toward European culture, as one who belongs to what you called "οι βαρβαροι," the barbarians?

---

1. E. Pound, *Cantos* ("The Pisan Cantos") LXXXIII.
2. E. Pound, "A Pact" (in *Lustra*, 1926).

When you came to Gibraltar from America, did you feel like one of these "οι βαρβαροι" arriving in Europe?

POUND I don't think I had as a young man any inferiority complex. My arrival at Gibraltar in 1908 was not a first visit, but a return. I'd been in Europe as a boy of twelve, as I wrote in "Indiscretions," an autobiographical piece about my early years.

PASOLINI I say this because, after reading your essays—fine literary essays—in spite of their profound erudition and the immense critical acumen they contain, there's something barbarous about them.

POUND My prose did in fact become crude during a certain period. It was a reaction, perhaps, to mixing with a respectable entourage.

PASOLINI "Eat of it not in the underworld, / See the sun or the moon bless thy eating, / κορη, κορη, for the six seeds of an error, / or that the stars bless thy eating, / o Lynx, guard this orchard, / keep from Demeter's furrow, / this fruit has a fire within it, / Pomona, Pomona, / No glass is clearer than the pomegranate body, / holding the flame? / Pomona, Pomona, / Lynx, keep watch on this orchard / that is named Melagrana, / or the Pomegranate field, / The sea is not clearer in azure, / nor the Heliads bringing light / here are lynxes, here are lynxes, / Is there a sound in the forest / of pard or of bassarid / or crotale or of leaves moving? / Cythera, here are the lynxes, / will the scrub-oak burst into flower? / There is a rose vine in this underbrush. / Red? White? No, but a colour between them / when the pomegranate is open and the light falls / half through it. / Lynx, beware of these vine-thorns / o Lynx, δλαυχωπιζ, coming up from the olive yards, / Kuthera, here are Lynxes and the clicking of crotales / there is a stir of dust from old leaves / will you trade roses for acorns, / will Lynxes eat thorn leaves?"[3]

I'll read these lines: "Under white clouds, cielo di Pisa, / out of all this beauty something must come."[4]

POUND They are good lines.

PASOLINI Yes, very good. Among your best.

POUND But good lines in my work are sparse. I didn't succeed in putting them in a cosmos.

PASOLINI No, I don't believe that. I think your poetry resembles life. You say your poetry is like speech between intelligent people. It follows a random, casual curve, with some sublime moments and others that are grey. In my view, your poetry follows this arc, so it isn't true that your best verses are not synthesized. . . .

POUND One tries to give them coherence, and one doesn't succeed.

PASOLINI Let one reader say that you did succeed. Do you think this "randomness" means letting beauty give birth to more beauty, on its own?

---

3. E. Pound, *Cantos* ("The Pisan Cantos") LXXIX.
4. E. Pound, *Cantos* ("The Pisan Cantos") LXXXIV.

POUND You honor me with your trust.

PASOLINI When you write, is your situation similar to that of the surrealists who write? That is, do you let the inspiration, the word, the language, come out almost automatically, or do you write very slowly, weighing one word at a time?

POUND I missed out on that.

PASOLINI All critics are in agreement that your poetry is enormously vast. It's as if your poems covered the surface of an immense poetic territory. And this is true, one quotation after another. . . .

POUND They're made at random.

PASOLINI What are at random? The criticisms or the quotations?

POUND They're made at random, they say, but it isn't true. They're musical, musical themes that recur.

PASOLINI This critical judgment seems right to me. Your poetry is enormously vast, but it's a first impression. Reading it better, all the elements that make it so vast in a certain sense become smaller. For example, to a reader like me, who's unfamiliar with Chinese literature and wisdom, all the Chinese quotations become *flatus vocis*, which are reduced to one element. The same for the Provençal poets' citations, or the Italian *dolce stil novo* poets, and so on; they too are reduced to just one element. While at first your poetry seems to cover a vast territory, gradually, however, it gets deeper. Instead of imagining you spreading over a vast linguistic territory, I see you at the bottom of a well in which you've reduced the world to a few elements: a group of citations that are always the same, a group of friends who return and are always the same, Yeats, Eliot. . . . I see you at the bottom of this narrow well in which you look back and reflect on your life.

POUND You're going deep and it's hard to reply from the surface where I am now.

PASOLINI "In 'The Spring and Autumn' there are no righteous wars."[5] And then: "Why wars? Said the sergeant rum-runner. Too many people, when they're too many, you must kill a few of them." They're pacifist verses. Would you like to take part in one of those demonstrations for peace that happen in America or in Italy?

POUND I believe in the good intentions, but not in the usefulness of these demonstrations. I look from another viewpoint, as I wrote in an unfinished Canto: "When one's friends hate each other, how can there be peace in the world?"[6]

PASOLINI What's the meaning of these lines I quoted: "In *The Spring and Autumn* there are no righteous wars." What is the meaning of *The Spring and Autumn*?

---

5. E. Pound, *Cantos* ("The Pisan Cantos") LXXVIII.
6. E. Pound, *Cantos* from CXV.

POUND They're the wings, they are memories, history transmitted.

PASOLINI *The Spring and Autumn* is the title of a Chinese book? In the Chinese tradition?

POUND Yes. *The Spring and Autumn* is a book attributed by some to Confucius, who was notoriously anything but a warmonger.

PASOLINI You've never been to China?

POUND No.

PASOLINI Do you regret, in your life, to have never seen China, which has so inspired you?

POUND Yes, I'd always hoped to see China. It's too late now, who knows. . . ?

PASOLINI Confucius is one of the names that recur frequently in your poetry. I want to ask you this question, which is a problem for me: Confucius is basically the only religious reformer, the only great religious philosopher who wasn't religious. His philosophy was above all practical, almost secular. I'd like to know how Confucius comes into your poetic world, which, though very secular in its cadence, is enormously religious in its irrationality, in its undecipherability.

POUND Perhaps I'd have tried to see the Confucian universe as a series of tensions.

PASOLINI One of the innumerable elements that make up the Cantos but are in reality reduced to a small territory at the bottom of this well where you reassess your life, one of these elements is Italy. What appealed to you most at first? The landscape or the people?

POUND The old landscape is ruined by these roads, where earth is changed for asphalt.

PASOLINI Italy at that time was still preindustrial, agrarian, artisan. Today it's a nation that is largely industrialized, so it produces literary phenomena analogous to those that America or England produced in those times. Italy is now one of these industrialized nations, which are culturally advanced, and therefore is creating a new kind of literature typical of industrialized, bourgeois nations. In Italy there's a sort of avant-garde movement that often uses your name. Do you accept paternity for these movements?

POUND You speak of industrialized, and therefore culturally advanced nations. It's that "therefore" I don't accept.

It's difficult for me to reply to your question, because not only in an industrialized Italy has there been a great increase, as you yourself say, of these neo-avant-garde products, but throughout the world, and it's impossible for me to keep up to date or, I was about to say, to keep afloat.

PASOLINI Are you pleased that your name is used by the maker of these Italian neo-avant-garde products, or not?

POUND If your theory of the old exile down in the dark well, reassessing his past life, is exact—I don't agree, yet maybe you are right—I wouldn't be in the position to see clearly what's happening outside, under the neon lights of the neo-world of the neo-avant-gardists, who I hope will understand and forgive those who can't see them.

PASOLINI Who are the painters you liked most?

POUND I think those of the quattrocento.

PASOLINI And among your contemporaries? Those who were working from '17 to '30, when you were young?

POUND Léger.

PASOLINI Did you like most the painters whose work resembled your poetry, or painters who belonged to a different world?

POUND I once wrote in the margins of a letter to the painter Wyndham Lewis: "I'm not very interested in painters." In fact, one critic wrote of me: "Pound chooses music and sculpture to compare them to poetry and has never shown a special interest in painting."

PASOLINI The second of your Pisan Cantos begins thus: "Out of Phlegethon, / out of Phlegethon, / Gerhart / are thou come forth out of Phlegethon? / With Buxtehude and Klages in your satchel, with the / Ständebuch of Sachs in your luggage / —not of one bird but of many."[7] Here the poem stops and a musical score follows.

POUND There were the first bars of this score, not the rest. There's too much.

PASOLINI What music is it?

POUND This "Song of the Birds" is by Jannequin, written for a choir. Francesco da Milano transcribed it for lute and Gherard retranscribed it for violin.

PASOLINI I'll read two verses which, I believe, concern your life. You wrote them in the Pisan Cantos, at a moment that was very painful in your life. "The young Dumas weeps because the young Dumas has tears."[8] Did you think of yourself as the "young Dumas"?

POUND No, with "the young Dumas" I was not thinking of myself. Indeed, in one of the Pisan Cantos I wrote: "*Tard, très tard je t'ai connue, la tristesse*" (Late, too late I met you, sadness).[9]

PASOLINI "What thou lov'st well shall not be reft from thee, / what thou lov'st well is thy true heritage, / whose world, or mine or theirs / or is it on none? / First came the seen, then the palpable / Elysium, though it were in the halls of hell, / what thou lovest well is thy true heritage / pull down thy vanity, it is not

---

7. E. Pound, *Cantos* ("The Pisan Cantos") LXXV.
8. E. Pound, *Cantos* ("The Pisan Cantos") LXXX.
9. E. Pound, *Cantos* ("The Pisan Cantos") LXXX.

man / made courage, or made order, or made grace, / pull down thy vanity, I say pull down / learn of the green world what can be thy place, / in scaled invention or true artistry, / pull down thy vanity, Pasquin, pull down! / The green casque has outdone your elegance. / "Master thyself, then others shall thee beare." / Pull down thy vanity / Thou art a beaten dog beneath the hail, / a swollen magpie in a fitful sun, / half black half white, / nor knowst'ou wing from tail / pull down thy vanity / how mean thy hates / fostered in falsity, / pull down thy vanity / rathe to destroy, niggard in charity, / pull down thy vanity, / I say pull down! / But to have done instead of not doing / this is not vanity. / To have, with decency, knocked that a Blunt should open, / to have gathered from the air a live tradition, / or from a fine old eye the unconquered flame, / this is not vanity. / Here error is all in the not done, / all in the diffidence that faltered."[10]

This interview took place in the fall of 1967 and was broadcast by RAI on June 19, 1968, in a program directed by Vanni Ronsisvalle, "An Hour with Ezra Pound." Quotations from Pound's Cantos, *courtesy of New Directions.*

---

10. E. Pound, *Cantos* ("The Pisan Cantos") LXXXI.

THE HIPPIES' SPEECH

The first time I saw the hippies was in Prague. In the hall of a hotel where I was staying two young foreigners entered with their long hair past their shoulders. They passed through the hall, reached a secluded corner, and sat at a table. They remained there for half an hour, observed by the other customers, among them myself, and then they took off. Neither, while passing through the customers in the hall and while sitting in their secluded corner, said a word (maybe—even if I do not remember it—they whispered something, but, I suppose, something very practical and unexpressive). In that particular situation—which was totally public, or social, and I would say "official"—they did not need to talk. Their silence was rigorously functional. It was that way simply because the spoken word was useless. The two of them used another language than the one of words to communicate with the customers.

What was substituting for traditional verbal language, making it useless—and finding an immediate collocation in the world of "signs," in the realm of semiology—was *the language of their hair*. It was a single sign—the length of their hair—in which all the possible signs of an articulate language were concentrated. What was the meaning of their silent and exclusively physical message?

It was this: "We are two hippies, we belong to a new human category that is appearing on the face of the earth these days, and that has its center in America, while in the provinces (like, for example—actually, above all—Prague) it is ignored. So for you we are an apparition. We bring forward our apostolate, already full of knowledge, that fulfills and exhausts us completely. We have nothing more to add orally or rationally to what physically and ontologically our hair is saying. The knowledge that fulfills us will one day belong to you too, also thanks to our apostolate. For now it is a novelty, a big Novelty, that creates in the world a scandal, a waiting, which will not be betrayed. The bourgeois are right to look at us with hatred and terror, because the essence itself of the length of our hair challenges them. But they should not think about us as impolite and wild people; we are aware of our responsibility. We don't look at you, we remain among ourselves. You should do the same and wait for the Events."

I was the receiver of this message and I was also able to decode it: that language was without lexicon, without grammar, without syntax; it could be understood right away as well, because, from a semiotic point of view, it was nothing more than a form of that "body language" that humans have been using since day one.

I understood and I felt an immediate antipathy for the two guys.

Then I regretted it, and defended the hippies from the attacks of the police and the fascists: I was, in principle, on the side of the Living Theatre, the Beats, etc., and the principle that made me stand by them was a rigorously democratic one.

The hippies became quite numerous, like the first Christians, but they kept being mysteriously silent; their long hair was their one true language, and it was not important to add anything else to it. Their speaking was their being. Their ineffability was the rhetorical art of their protest.

What were the hippies of '66–'67 saying with the inarticulate language that consists of the monolithic sign of hair?

They were saying this: "We are fed up with this world made out of consumerism. We protest in a radical way. We are creating an antibody against this world through refusal. Everything seems to go for the best, eh? Our generation should have been integrated? But instead here is how things really are. We oppose madness to a destiny made of 'executives.' We create new religious values in the bourgeois entropy, exactly when it was about to become perfectly secular and hedonistic. We are doing it with a revolutionary violence (the violence of nonviolents!) because our critique towards our society is total and intransigent."

I do not think that if interviewed according to traditional verbal language, they would be capable of expressing their "hair point of view" in such an articulate way: but this is substantially what they were saying. As for me, even though I was suspecting that their sign system was produced by a subculture of protest that was opposing a subculture of power, and that their non-Marxist revolution was also suspect, I continued to be on their side for a while, taking them at the least as an anarchic element of my own ideology.

The language of their hair was expressing leftist "stuff," maybe of the New Left, born inside the bourgeois universe (in a dialectic created maybe artificially by the Mind that regulates, outside the conscience of historical and particular Powers, the destiny of the bourgeoisie).

1968 came. The hippies were absorbed by the Student Movement, they were carrying red flags on the barricades. The language was expressing more and more leftist "stuff" (Che Guevara had long hair, etc.).

In 1969—with the Milan killings,[1] the mafia, the emissaries

---

1. In Piazza Fontana in Milan, a bomb killed 17 and wounded 88. As usual, communists and the Left were accused. But though the terrorists never have been identified or condemned, the slaughter is believed to have been the work of the fascists and right-wing anarchists.

of the Greek colonels,[2] the complicity of ministers, the fascist plot, the provocateurs—the hippies started to spread: even if they were not the majority in terms of numbers, in reality they were, because of the specific ideological weight they had. Now the hippies were not silent anymore: they were not delegating their capacity to communicate and express themselves to the sign system of their hair. On the contrary, the physical presence of the hair was, in a certain sense, downgraded to a distinctive function. The verbal language came back. And I am not saying language by pure chance. We spoke a lot from 1968 to 1970, we spoke so much that for a while we can afford to even avoid speaking: we used verbality to the limits, and verbalism was the new rhetoric of the revolution (gauchisme,[3] the verbal disease of Marxism!).

Even if the hair—absorbed by the fury of the verbal language—was no longer speaking autonomously to the receivers, I found the strength to improve my decoding capacities anyway, and in the madness I tried to listen to the silent speech of that hair, which by then was growing and growing.

What was it saying now? It was saying: "Yes, it's true, I'm saying leftist stuff; my meaning is a leftist meaning. But. . . . But. . . ."

The speech of the long hair was stopping here: I had to complete it myself. With that "But" it wanted to say two things: 1) "My ineffability reveals itself more and more as one of the irrational and pragmatic kind: the pre-eminence that I silently attribute to the action is of a subcultural sort, therefore mainly of the right wing; 2) I have also been adopted by the fascist

---

2. The "colonels" refers to the Greek military junta that ruled Greece through the '60s and only came apart with the student Polytechnic Revolt in 1973.

3. That is, leftism.

provocateurs, who have blended with the verbal revolutionaries (the verbalism can also lead to action, especially when it mythifies it): and I constitute a perfect mask, not only from the physical point of view—my chaotic flowing tends to make every face similar—but also from the cultural point of view: in fact a right-wing subculture can easily be confused with a leftist subculture."

So I understood that the language of the long hair was no longer expressing "leftist things" but instead something quite equivocal, a Right-Left, that was making the presence of the provocateurs possible.

Ten years ago I was thinking that among ourselves of the previous generations, a provocateur was almost inconceivable (unless he was a great actor): in fact his subculture would have distinguished itself, *even physically*, from our subculture. We would have recognized him from the eyes, the nose, *the hair!* We would have taken away his mask and we would have given him the lesson he deserved. Now this is no longer possible. Nowadays no one could ever distinguish, from the physical presence, a revolutionary from a provocateur. Left and Right have physically merged.

We arrived at 1972.

This past September I was in the city of Isfahan, in the heart of Persia, an undeveloped country, as they horribly say, but ready to fly, as they also horribly say.

On the Isfahan of 10 years ago—one of the most beautiful cities of the world, if not the most beautiful—a new Isfahan has been born, modern and very ugly. But on its streets, at work, or while walking, towards dawn, one could see the boys that one used to see in Italy 10 years ago: sons full of dignity, and humble, with their beautiful heads, their beautiful faces under innocent hair. One night, while walking on the main road, I saw two monstrous beings among all those ancient and beautiful boys full of human dignity: they were not really hippies, but they were showing off a European haircut: long on their shoulders, short in front, sticky because of the artificial stuff they put on.

What was that hair saying? It was saying "I do not belong to those bums, those poor underdeveloped guys, stuck in the middle ages. I am a bank worker, a student, the son of people who need to make money and who now work for the gas industry, I know Europe, I read, I am a bourgeois and here is my hair that testifies to my international modernity of the privileged kind."

That long hair was hinting at right-wing "stuff." The cycle is concluded. The subculture in power absorbed the subculture that was in opposition and took possession of it with devilish ability, and passionately made of it a fashion that, if we cannot really call it fascist in the classic sense of the word, is after all extremely right-wing.

To bitterly conclude: the horrible masks that the young people put on their faces to make themselves dirty like the old whores of an unjust iconography, objectively recreate on their features that which they only verbally had condemned forever. The old looks of priests, of judges, of officials, and fake anarchists, fool clerks, mercenaries, crooks, and gangsters came out. Meaning: the radical sentence that they pronounced against their fathers—who are the history in evolution and the preceding culture—by raising against them an insuperable barrier, ended up isolating them, preventing them from a dialectical relationship with their fathers. Now, only through this dialectic relationship—even if it is extreme and dramatic—could they have had an oral historical consciousness of the self, and they would have moved on, "exceeded." On the other hand, the isolation in which they closed themselves—like a world apart, in a ghetto reserved for youth—kept them still at their historical reality: and this implied, fatally, a regression. In truth, compared to their fathers, they went back, resuscitating in their soul terrors and conformism, and in their physical appearance conventionality and miseries that had appeared to have been gone forever.

Now the long hair is saying, in its inarticulate and obsessed language of non-verbal signs, in its vandal symbolism, the "things" of TV and commercials, where it is now inconceivable to foresee a young person without long hair, something that nowadays would be a scandal for the power in charge.

I feel a deep and endless pain (I'd say a desperation) in saying this, but now thousands and hundreds of thousands of young Italians resemble more and more the face of Merlin. Their freedom of having their hair as they like is no longer defensible, because it is not freedom anymore. The moment has come to say to the young people that the way they wear their hair is horrible, because it is servile and vulgar. The moment has come that they themselves should realize it and should free themselves from their anxious guilt in obeying the degrading order of the horde.

1973. Translated by Flavio Rizzo

NOTE ON POETRY DOWN SOUTH

So one can't go *forward* anymore.

Why have you let our kids be educated by the middle class? Why have you allowed our houses to be built by the middle class? Why have you tolerated our souls being tempted by the middle class? Why have you only verbally protested while, little by little, our culture was being transformed into a middle-class culture? Why have you accepted that our bodies would live as middle-class culture? Why haven't you risen up against our anxiety that daily justified itself by ripping off something from the poor to have a middle-class life? Why have you conducted yourselves in such a way as to find yourselves facing this *fait accompli* and seeing that, by now, there's nothing more to do, why are you inclined to save the savable, participating in middle-class power?

So one can't go *forward* anymore.

We'll need to turn back and re-begin all over again. So that our kids aren't educated by the middle class, so that our homes aren't constructed by the middle class, so that our souls aren't tempted by the middle class. So that if our culture couldn't and shouldn't any longer be the culture of poverty, it might be transformed into a communist culture. So that our bodies, if it's fated that they no longer live out the innocence and mystery of poverty, might live as communist culture. So that our anxiety, if it's no longer an anxiety due to misery, might be an anxiety for necessary goods.

Let's turn back with clenched fists, and re-begin all over again. You won't find yourselves facing the fait accompli of a middle-class power destined by now to be eternal. Your problem won't be the problem of saving the savable. No compromise! Let's turn back. Long live poverty. Long live the communist struggle for necessary goods.

1974. Translated by Jack Hirschman

THE POWER WITHOUT A FACE:
THE TRUE FASCISM AND THEREFORE
THE TRUE ANTIFASCISM

What is the *culture* of a nation? Commonly it's believed, even by *cultured* people, that it's the *culture* of the scientists, of the politicians, of the literary men, of the filmmakers, etc.: namely, that it's the *culture* of the *intelligentsia*. But this is rather untrue. It's not even the *culture* of the ruling class that tries to impose it, at least formally, precisely through the class struggle. And finally it's not even the *culture* of the ruled class, meaning the popular *culture* of the workers and the peasants.

The culture of a nation is the drawing together of all these class cultures: it's the average of all of them. And it would be an abstract concept if it were not recognizable or—to say this better—visible in the living and existential experience, and consequently if it didn't maintain a practical dimension. For many centuries, in Italy, these cultures have been distinguishable even if historically unified. Today—almost suddenly as some sort of Advent—historical distinction and historical unification have ceded their place to a homologation that almost miraculously fulfills the inter-classistic dream of the old Power. What causes such homologation? Clearly it's a new Power.

I'm writing "Power" with capital P—a use for which Maurizio Ferrara[1] has accused me of irrationalism in *L'Unità* (6/12/1974)—only because I sincerely don't know what such

---

1. A great antifascist. Secretary to Palmiro Togliatti (1893–1964), head of the Communist Party.

Power consists of and who represents it. I simply know that it exists. I no longer recognize it in the Vatican, neither in the powerful Christian Democrats, nor in the Army. I no longer recognize it even in big business because it no longer employs a limited number of big-time industrialists; I think that big business appears in fact as a "whole" (a total industrialization), and mostly as a "non-Italian whole" (transnational).

I also recognize—because I see them and live them—certain characteristics of this new faceless Power: for instance, its rejection of the old Sanfedism[2] and the old Clericalism, its decision to abandon the Church, its determination (crowned with success) to transform the peasants and the underclass into petty-bourgeois, and, above all, its eagerness, cosmic so to speak, to carry out a "Development" at any cost, by producing and consuming.

The identikit of this new faceless Power vaguely assigns to it certain "modern" traits derived from tolerance and from a hedonistic ideology perfectly autonomous. But this identikit also assigns to this power ferocious and substantially repressive traits; the trait of tolerance is in fact false, because in reality there is no man who is supposed to be so normal and so conformist as the consumer, and, as for the hedonistic ideology, it clearly hides a decision to prearrange everything with a ruthlessness as yet unknown to history. Therefore, this new Power, not yet represented by anyone and caused by a "mutation" of the ruling class, is in reality—if we really want to keep the old terminology—a "total" form of fascism. But this new Power has also culturally homologated Italy: it is therefore a repressive homologation even though obtained by the imposition of a form

---

2. A reactionary clerical and anti-liberal tendency.

of hedonism and a *joie de vivre*. State Terror gives an inkling, even if substantially anachronistic, of all this.

Maurizio Ferrara, in his aforementioned article, accuses me of aestheticism (as does Ferrarotti[3] in *Paese Sera*, 6/14/1974). And with this he tends towards my exclusion and reclusion. That's fine. My perspective could be that of an "artist," namely, as the good bourgeoisie wants it, that of an insane person. But the fact that, for instance, two representatives of the old Power (though in reality they now serve, even if in an interlocutory fashion, the new Power) blackmailed one another regarding the financing for the Parties and the Montesi case,[4] would be enough to drive someone insane; that is, discrediting a ruling class and the society before the eyes of a man with such intensity as to induce him to lose any sense of opportunity and limits, consequently throwing him into an actual state of "anomie." It needs to be said that the view of the insane person is to be taken into serious consideration, unless one decides to be progressive in everything except the problem of the insane person, limiting his own effort by conveniently removing him.

There are certain insane people who watch others' faces and behavior, not because they are epigones of a "Lombrosian"[5] positivism (as Ferrara has coarsely defined it) but because they know Semiology. They know that culture produces codes, that codes produce behavior, that behavior is a language, and that in a historical moment when verbal language is completely

---

3. Franco Ferraroti, left-wing sociologist.
4. Refers to the murder of Wilma Montesi, 21, a young Roman woman. At first called a suicide, the unsolved case soon involved politicians and members of the Italian aristocracy close to fascism.
5. Cesare Lombroso, a 19th-century criminologist, developed a theory that criminal and violent attitudes were hereditarily tied to somatic characteristics.

conventional and sterilized (technicalized), the language of behavior (physical and gestural) assumes crucial importance.

Coming back to the beginning of our talk, it seems to me that there are good reasons to maintain that the culture of a nation (in this case Italy) is today expressed mostly through the language of behavior, or physical language, in addition to a certain amount—completely conventionalized and extremely poor—of verbal language.

This aforementioned culture is at such a level of linguistic communication that the following manifestations occur: a) the anthropological transformation of the Italian people; b) their complete homologation into one single model.

Therefore, deciding to let the hair grow down to the shoulders, or cutting the hair and growing mustaches (echoing 19th-century style), deciding to wear a headband or to pull the hat down over the eyes, deciding whether to dream of a Ferrari or a Porsche, following television programs attentively, knowing the titles of a few bestsellers, wearing overbearingly fashionable pants and T-shirts, having obsessive relationships with girls kept as ornaments at one's side but at the same time demanding their freedom, etc., etc., etc.—all of these examples are *cultural* acts.

Now, every young Italian performs these identical acts, they have this type of physical language, they are interchangeable; this is a thing as old as the world, if considered limited to a single social class or to a category. But the fact is that these cultural acts and this somatic language are inter-classist. No one will ever be able to distinguish, in a square full of people, a worker from a student, a fascist from an antifascist, by way of their bodies—something that was still possible in 1968.

The problems of an intellectual who belongs to the intelligentsia are different from the ones of a political party and of a man of politics, even if the ideology is perhaps the same. I would like my current leftist opponents to understand I am capable of realizing that, if the leftist parties would not support the Power in force, if in fact Economic Development underwent a standstill and a recession, Italy would simply fall to pieces; but if instead Economic Growth continued as well as when it began, the so-called "historic compromise," the only way to try to correct Economic Growth (as indicated by Berlinguer[6] in his report at the Central Committee of the Communist Party) would be undoubtedly realistic. However, in the same way, the issue of "faces" should not be of Maurizio Ferrara's concern, and this political practice's maneuver should not be my concern. Actually, I have, if anything, the duty to exercise my "Don Quixotean" and extremist critique on it. Therefore what are my problems?

Here is one for example. In the article that generated this controversy (*Corriere della Sera*, 6/10/1974), I claim that the true responsible parties in the Milano and Brescia massacres[7] are the government and the Italian police, because had they wanted to, the government and the police could have prevented the two massacres from taking place. This is rather commonplace. Well, at this point I will allow anyone to laugh behind my back by saying that we, progressives, antifascists, and leftists, are also responsible for these massacres. In fact we have done nothing in all these years:

---

6. Enrico Berlinguer, 1922–1984. He was the national Secretary of the Italian Communist Party (PCI) from 1972 until his death.

7. In Brescia in 1974, during an antifascist trade-union demonstration, a bomb killed eight people and wounded 100. As in the Milan massacre, there were no convictions, though three of the accused were members of a neo-fascist party.

1) to prevent the talk around "State Massacre" from becoming a commonplace and to prevent it from stopping and not going any further; and

2) (what is even more serious) we have done nothing because the fascists were not us. We limited ourselves to condemning them, gratifying our own conscience with our indignation; and the stronger and the more insistent was our indignation, the clearer was our conscience.

In reality, we have acted with the fascists (I'm mostly speaking of the young fascists) as racists: we, as racists, have hastily and ruthlessly believed that they were predestined to be fascists and, confronted with this decision, we believed that there was nothing to be done about their fate. Let's not hide this fact: we were all aware in our true conscience, that when one of our young made the casual decision to be a fascist, it was a groundless and irrational gesture. A word could have been enough to prevent this from happening. But none of us ever spoke with them or to them. We immediately accepted them as representatives of Evil. Maybe they were eighteen-year-old young adolescents who didn't know anything about anything and they rushed headlong into any horrible adventure simply out of desperation.

But we could not have distinguished them from the others (I don't mean from the other extremists: but from ALL others). This is our dreadful justification.

Father Zosima[8] was able to distinguish immediately, from those who had crowded into his cell, the parricide Dmitri

---

8. Father Zosima is the sage Russian monk in Dostoyevsky's *The Brothers Karamazov.*

Karamazov. He got up from his chair and prostrated himself before him. And he did it (as he later confessed to the younger Karamazov) because Dmitri was destined to carry out the most horrible act and to suffer the most inhuman pain.

Think (if you have the strength) about that young person or persons who went to place the bombs in the square of Brescia. Shouldn't we have prostrated ourselves before them? But they were young and with long hair, or they had early-19th-century-style mustaches, they wore a headband or a hat down over the eyes, they were pale and conceited, their concern was to dress up fashionably, all in the same manner, to have a Porsche or a Ferrari, or a motorcycle to drive like little archangel idiots with their decorative girls on the back—decorative, yes, but modern and in favor of divorce, of women's liberation, and in general of economic growth. . . . In short they were young people just like others: nothing distinguished them in any way.

Even if we wanted to, we would not have been able to prostrate ourselves before them. The old fascism, even if with rhetorical degeneration, made people distinguishable, but the new fascism—which is anything but that—no longer makes distinction possible: it is not humanistically rhetorical, but pragmatic in the American way.

Its goal is the brutally totalitarian reorganization and homologation of the world.

1974. Translated by Veruska Cantelli

POEMS 1941–1963

ODE TO A FLOWER IN CASARSA

Desert flower, flowers from the garland
of our houses where families
bicker in the open air,

you browse on the stones of the day,
simple, while field and sky
like sky and sea
appear all around.

Rustic desert flower,

no evening streaming with lights.

No shepherds drenched by dew,

slender fire of the hedges.

No marsh-marigold, bilberry, swamp-violet
or Florentine iris, or gentian, no angelica,
no Parnassian grass or marsh-myrtle.

You're Pieruti, Zuan
and tall Bepi with his walking-sticks of bone,
slim at the helm of his wagon,

pasture flower.

You become hay. Burn, burn,
sun of my town, little desert flower.

The years pass over you,
and so do I, with the shadow of the acacia tree,
with the sunflower, on this quiet day.

1941. Translated by Jack Hirschman

THE CORAN TESTAMENT[1]

In the year 1944
I was the Botèrs' servant;
ours was a holy time
burnt by the sun of chores.
Black clouds in the fireplace,
white stains in the sky
were the fear and pleasure
in loving the hammer and sickle.

I was a 16-year-old boy
with a rough, untidy heart,
my eyes hot-red roses,
my hair like my mother's.
I started playing bocce-ball,
greasing my curls, dancing on Sundays.
Black shoes! white shirts!
Youth, O foreign country!

At that time we hunted frogs
at night with a light and fishing spear.
Rico bloodied the reeds
and weeds with a red lamp,
in shadows frosting our bones.
In the Sile River thousands of

---

1. Not a reference to the Islamic book but the family name of the teenage narrator.

small fish swam in the paddies.
We walked slowly, without a cry.

In the small poplar wood
after having eaten, the gang of boys
would gather together and
often we cursed
and sang like birds.
Then we played cards
in the shadow of the cornstalks.
Momma and poppa had died.

Sundays us tough little guys
rode off on our bikes
to priceless enchanting places.
One evening, in the light
of the woods, I saw Neta,
pasturing her sheep.
With her stick
she stirred the silken air.

I smelled of grass and manure
and of the sweat resigned
to my warm leathery chest;
and my pants, tied 'round
my waist, forgotten by dawn,
couldn't hide the swollen desire
for dreamy sunrises and evenings
without the cool rains.

For the first time I tried
with that 13-year-old girl;
full of passion I ran away
to tell my friends about it.
It was Saturday, one couldn't
see even a dog on the streets.
The Sellàns' house was burning.
All the lights were off.

In the middle of the square was a
dead man in a puddle of frozen blood.
In that village deserted as the sea,
four Germans captured me
and furiously screaming
pushed me into a van closed in shadow.
After three days they hanged me
from the tavern's mulberry tree.

I bequeath my image to
the conscience of the rich:
my empty eyes, my clothes
smelling of my rough sweat
With the Germans I wasn't scared
of leaving my youth.
Long live the courage and the sorrow
and the innocence of the poor!

1948–49. Translated from Friulian By Lucia Gazzino

LET'S UNITE!

Day after day I went on living
alone with my sorrows:
born poor, I died
day after day: evil is bottomless.

Sin—I don't know if I'm a sinner,
but I've not even died of love.
In the shadow the aching sinew
of my pity grew weary.

Shameful, we believe without soul
in misery and in God,
our lives are teeming rivers
and we've no words left to speak.

I was alone, so was your mother
and now, grandson, it's you
swallowing poverty, the blowing
bora-wind, a soup that won't go down.

Let's unite! The cloud will become rain,
the seed turn into wheat,
the spring become a brook:
the poor will become conscious.

Let's unite! Spring's on the way;
from the corpse, flowers will bloom;

we are the corpses, Springtime,
a thousand hearts sprouting Love !

Let's unite! The Animal's spoken,
distant lands are drawing near,
the slave's unchained himself:
poor people will get back their souls!

1949. Translated from Friulian by Lucia Gazzino

A DESPERATE VITALITY

I

(Draft, in cursus—in the direction—through the use of current jargon, of a previous occurrence: Fiumicino, the old castle, and a first insight into the reality of death.)

As in a film by Godard:[1] alone
in a car moving along the highways
of Latin neo-capitalism—returning from the airport—
[that's where Moravia remained, pure among his luggage]
    alone, "at the wheel of his Alfa Romeo"
       beneath a sun so divine
       indescribable in non-elegiac rhyme
       —the most beautiful sun of the year—
as in a film by Godard:
       beneath that unique sun that steadily bled,
       the canal of Fiumicino's port
       —a motorboat returning unnoticed
       —Neapolitan sailors in their woolen rags
       —a highway accident with only a small crowd around . . .
—as in a film by Godard—
rediscovered romanticism contained
in cynical neo-capitalism, and cruelty—
at the wheel
on the road to Fiumicino,
and there's the castle (sweet

---

1. A reference to Godard's film *Contempt* (*Le mépris*, 1963).

mystery, for the French screenwriter,
in the troubled, infinite, secular sun,

this papal beast, with its battlements,
on the hedges and vine rows of the ugly
countryside of peasant serfs) . . .

—I'm like a cat burned alive,
run over by the wheels of a truck,
hung from a fig tree by boys,

but with at least eight of
its nine lives intact;
like a snake reduced to bloody pulp,
a half-eaten eel

—sunken cheeks defining tired eyes,
hair horribly thinned out against the skull,
skinny arms, like those of a child
—Belmondo, a cat that never dies,
"at the wheel of his Alfa Romeo"
in the logic of narcissistic montage,
detaches himself from time, and inserts
Himself:
into images that have nothing to do with
the boredom of the progressing hours . . .
the slow dying glitter of the afternoon . . .

Death lies not
in being unable to communicate,
but in the failure to continue being understood.

And this papal beast, not lacking
grace—the reminder
of rustic landlord concessions,
innocent, after all,
as was the serfs' resignation—
in the sun that was,
in the centuries,
for thousands of afternoons,
here, the only guest,

this papal beast, with battlements
crouching amid marsh poplars,
melon fields, banks,

this papal beast protected
by buttresses of the sweet orange color
of Rome, ruined
like Roman or Etruscan buildings,

is at the point of no longer being understood.

II

*(No fade-out, a clean break, I portray myself in an act—with no
historical precedents—of "cultural industry")*

Me, voluntarily martyred . . . and
her across from me, on the sofa:
flashes back and forth, between positions,
"You" —I know what she's thinking, looking at me,

in the most domestic-Italian M.F.,[2]
always *à la* Godard—"you, Tennessee type!"
the cobra in the wool sweater
    (with the subordinate cobra
    skimming in magnesial silence).
Then loudly: "Will you tell me what you're writing?"

"Verses, verses, I'm writing verses!
(damned fool,
verses she's in no position to understand,
having no knowledge of metrics! Verses!)
verses   NO LONGER IN TRIPLETS!

      Understand?
That's the important thing: no longer in triplets!
I've gone back *tout court* to magma!
Neo-capitalism has won, I'm
out on the street
    as a poet, ah [sob]
    and as a citizen [another sob]."
And the man-cobra with the pen:
"The title of your work?" "I don't know . . .
[Then he talks in a low tone, fearful, resuming
the accepted role that the conversation imposes
on him: it takes nothing
to discolor

---

2. "M.F." has been subject to many interpretations. In the context of the Godardian scene, it likely stands for the Italian cinematographic term "mezza figura," a "half-bust" shot.

his grim face
into that of some poor fool condemned to die]
—maybe . . . 'The Persecution'
or . . . 'A New Prehistory' (or Prehistory)
or . . .
[At this point he becomes angry, regains
the dignity of civil hate]
    'Monologue on the Jews' . . ."
                  [The dialogue falls
like the weakness of the arsis
of mixed-up octosyllabic verses: magmatic!]
"And what is it about?"
"Well, about my . . . His, death.
It's not in the inability to communicate, [death]
but in the inability to be understood . . .

    (If only the cobra knew
    that it's a useless idea
    thought up on the way back from Fiumicino!)
They're almost all lyric verses, of which
the composition in time and place
consists, oddly!, of a ride in a car . . .
meditations from forty to eighty miles an hour . . .
with fast pans and tracking shots
to follow or precede
on significant monuments, or groups
of people, which spurn
an objective love . . . of citizen
(or street user) . . ."

"Ah, ah—[the she-cobra with the pen laughing]— . . .
who is it that doesn't understand?"
"Those who are no longer with us."

III

Those who are no longer with us!
Taken, with their innocent youth, by a new breath
of history, to other lives!

I remember it being . . . for a love
that invaded my brown eyes and honest trousers,
house and countryside, the morning sun and

the evening sun . . . during the good Saturdays
of the Friuli, during . . . Sundays . . . Ah!,
I can't even pronounce this word

of virgin passions, of my death (seen
in a dry ditch full with primroses,
between vineyard rows stunned by gold, near

farmhouses, dark against a sublime blue).

I remember that in the midst of that monstrous love
I would scream in pain
for the Sundays when it would have to shine

"over the sons of the sons, the sun!"

I cried, on the cot in Casarsa,
in the room that smelled of urine and laundry
those Sundays that shone to death . . .

Incredible tears! Not only for
what I was losing, in that moment
of wearing immobility of the splendor,

but for what I *would* lose! When
other youngsters—of whom I couldn't even think,
so similar to those who now dressed up,

wearing white socks and windbreakers,
with flowers in their lapels—or dark material,
for weddings, treated with filial tenderness,

—would populate the Casarsa of the future,
unchanged, with its stones, and the sun
that covered it with a dying golden shower . . .

With an epileptic impetus of homicidal pain
I protested,
like one condemned to life imprisonment,
by locking myself in
my room,
without anyone knowing it,
to scream, my mouth
blocked by sheets darkened
by the heat of an iron,
the sheets of my family,

on which I'd brood over the flower
of my youth.

And once, after dinner, or maybe it was night,
I ran, screaming
through Sunday streets, after the game,
to the old cemetery, behind the train tracks,
to carry out and repeat, down to the blood,
the sweetest act in life,
alone there on a pile of the dirt
of two or three graves
of Italian or German soldiers
with no names on the wooden crosses
—buried there since the other war.

And, that night, amid dry tears,
the bloody bodies of those unknowns
dressed in green-gray rags

came to cluster on my bed,
where I slept naked and empty,
to stain me with blood, till dawn.

I was twenty, not even—eighteen,
nineteen . . . and I'd been alive for a century,
a whole lifetime

consumed by the pain of the fact
that I'd never ever be able to give my love
if not to my hand, or to the grass of ditches

or maybe to the earth of an unguarded tomb . . .
Twenty and, with its human history and its cycle
of poetry, a life had ended.

IV

(*Resumption of the interview, and confused explanations on the
function of Marxism, etc.*)

(Ah, mine is but a visit to this world!)

But let's get back to reality.

[She's here, face visibly preoccupied but camouflaged by good
manners, waiting, in the "gray" frame, in accordance with the
good rules of French classicism. A Léger.]

"According to you then"—she says, reticent,
biting her pen—"what is the function
of a Marxist?" And gets ready to write.

"With . . . the delicacy of a bacteriologist . . . I would say
[overcome by the impetus of death, I stutter]
to move masses the size of Napoleonic and Stalinist armies . . .
with millions of extensions . . .
in such a manner that . . .
the masses which consider themselves conservative
[re: the Past] would lose it:
revolutionary masses would acquire it,
rebuild it through the act of defeating it . . .
I am a Communist as a result of

the instinct of Preservation!
A shift
on which depend life and death: in the centuries of the
centuries.

To do it very carefully, like when
a bomb-squad captain undoes the safety
from a live bomb and, for a moment
his existence (in a world of modern buildings
in the sun) remains undecided:

an inconceivable disproportion
between the horns!
A shift
to be made slowly, stretching the neck,
bending, tightening one's stomach,
biting one's lips or closing one's eyes
like a lawn bowler
who, when bowling, tried to dominate
the course of his shot, to rectify it
toward a solution
that will designate life through the centuries."

V

Life, through the centuries . . .
That's what it was getting at
last night . . .
benumbed in the briefness of its wail—
that distant train . . .

That train that wailed
discouraged; as if astonished at its existence,
(and, at the same time, resigned—because every act
of life is a segment extant in a line
that is life itself, clear only in dreams)

that train wailed and its wailing
—unimaginably far, passed the Appias
and the Centocelle[3] of the world—
united itself to another act:
casual union, monstrous, odd
and so very private
that only beyond the line of my perhaps closed eyes
is it possible to know it . . .

Mine was an act of love. But lost in the misery
of a body granted by a miracle,
in the exhaustion of hiding, panting
along a dim railroad, stepping in the mud
of a countryside cultivated by giants . . .

Life through the centuries . . .
like a falling star
beyond the sky of gigantic ruins,
beyond the properties of the Caetani or the Torlonia,
beyond the Tuscolane and the Capannelle[4] of the world—
that mechanical wail said:
life through the centuries . . .

---

3. Appias and Centocelle are Roman zones.
4. Caetani, Torlonia, Tuscolane, and Capannelle are names of wealthy Italian familes, owners of large villas.

And my senses were there, listening.

I was caressing a ruffled and dusty head,
blond, like the color one needs in life,
of the design of destiny,
and a colt's body, tender and agile,
with rough canvas clothes knowing of a mother's care:
I was making love,
but my senses were listening to:

life through the centuries . . .

The blond head of destiny disappeared
through a hole,
in the hole was the night sky,
until, against that edge of sky, appeared
another head of hair,
black, or maybe dark brown: and I,
in the cave lost in the heart of the estates
of the Caetani or the Torlonia
among ruins built by giants of the 1600s
during immense carnival days, I,
with my senses, was listening to . . .

life through the centuries . . .

Again and again, in the hole, against the whiteness
of the night losing itself
beyond the Casiline[5] of the world,

---

5. Another Roman area.

the head of destiny appeared and disappeared,
now with the sweetness of a southern mother,
now of an alcoholic father, always the same head,
ruffled and dusty, or already set
in the vanity of everyday youth:
and I,
I was listening with my senses to

the clearest voice of another love
—life through the centuries—
that was rising in the sky.

VI

(*A fascist victory*)

She looks at me in pity.
"And . . . but then you . . . —[mundane smile, greedy,
conscious of the greed and captivating
ostentatiousness—flaming eyes and teeth—
of a slightly hesitant childish contempt
toward herself]—but then you're very unhappy!"

"Well, Miss, (I have to admit it)
I'm in a state of confusion.

Re-reading my typewritten book
of poetry (this, the one we're talking about)
I had a vision . . . oh, if only
just a chaos of contradictions—reassuring
contradictions . . . No, it's the vision

of a confused soul . . .

Every false sentiment
produces the absolute certainty of having it.
My false sentiment was that . . .
of health. Strange! By telling her
—unsympathetic by definition,
with that lipless doll's face—
I verified with clinical clarity
the fact
that I'd never possessed any clarity.

It's true that at times it's enough
to be sane (and clear)
to believe it . . . Nevertheless
(write, write!) my actual confusion
is a consequence
of a fascist victory.
        [new, uncontrolled,
        loyal death impulses]
A small, secondary victory.
Easy, then. I was alone:
with my bones, a shy frightened
mother, and my will.

The objective was to humiliate one who was
humiliated. I must tell you that they succeeded,
and without much effort. Maybe
if they'd known how easy it was they wouldn't
have tried as hard, and in such great numbers!

(Ah, you see, I talk in a generic plural: They!
with the beckoning love the madman has for his sickness.)

The results of this victory, they too,
then, count very little: one less
authoritative signature in the appeals for peace.
Well, objects aside, it's not much—0.
Subjects aside . . . But let's forget it:
I've described too much,
and never orally,
my pains of a squashed worm
that holds up its little head and debates
with repugnant ingenuity, etc.

A fascist victory!
Write, write: they should know that I know:

with the conscience of a wounded bird
that, meekly dying, does not forgive."

VII

Does not forgive!

There was a soul, among those
that were to descend into life
—many, and all similar, poor souls—,
a soul in whose brown eyes of light,
in the modest wave of hair combed
by a mother's idea of masculine beauty,
burned the desire to die.

It was instantly seen,
by him who does not forgive.

He took it, called it to his side,
and, like an artisan,
up in the worlds that precede life,
placed his hands on its head
and pronounced the curse.

It was a candid and clean soul,
like a child at his first communion,
wise to the wisdom of his ten years,
dressed in white, of a material
chosen by a mother's idea of manly grace,
with eyes warm with the desire to die.

Oh, it was instantly seen,
by him who does not forgive.

He was the infinite capacity to obey
and the infinite capacity to rebel:
he called it to himself and worked on it
—while it looked at him with trust
like a lamb looks up at his butcher—
a reverse consecration,
while the light fell from his eyes
and a shadow of pity filled the space.

"You shall go into the world,
you shall be candid and gentle, stable, and faithful,
you shall have an infinite capacity to obey

and an infinite capacity to rebel.
You shall be pure.
Therefore, I curse you."

I can still see his eyes full of pity
and of the slight horror one feels
for the one who inspires it,
—the stare that follows
one who goes unknowingly to his death
and, out of a necessity that dominates
those who know and those who do not,
says nothing. I still see his stare,
as I moved away—from Eternity—
toward my cradle.

VIII

(Funereal conclusion: with synoptic table—for use by the writer
of the "piece"—of my career as poet, and a prophetic
look at the sea of future millennia.)

I came into the world at the time
of the Analogic.
Worked
in that field as apprentice.
Then there was the Resistance
and I
fought using poetry as a weapon.
I restored Logic,
and became a civic poet.
Now is the time

of Psychagogy.
I can only write prophecies
within the rapture of Music
resulting from an excess of sperm or pity.

*

"If now the Analogic survives
and Logic is out of style
(and I with it:)
there's no call for my poetry.
Psychagogy
remains
(in spite of Demagogy's
constant control
of the situation).
And thus
I'm able to write Themes and Threnodies
and even Prophecies;
oh, yes, always as a civil poet!"

*

"As to the future, listen:
its fascist sons
will sail
toward the worlds of the New Prehistory.
I'll be there
like one dreaming of his own damnation,
at the edge of the sea
in which life begins again.
Alone, or almost, on the ancient shore
among the remains of ancient civilizations.

Ravenna
Ostia, or Bombay—it's all the same—
with Gods picking their scabs of old problems
—such as class struggle—
which
dissolve . . .
Like a partisan
dead before May 1945,
I will slowly decompose
in the tormenting light of that sea,
a forgotten poet and citizen."

IX

(Escape Clause)

"My God, but then what assets
do you have? . . ."
"Me?—[nefariously stammering,
not having taken my medication,
my sickly boy's voice trembles]—
Me? A desperate vitality."

1964. Translated by Pasquale Verdicchio

BALLAD OF STALIN'S MOTHER

I, who was innocent, my son,
have given you the love of sin.
The fox born from the dove
comes in the night and eats up
the livestock of the poor.
In the centuries that we're slaves,
innocence makes parents more
children than their children, and masters
love them because they're so simon-pure.
The innocence of slaves isn't history!

My son, I who was mild
have given you a love of rancor.
The sun born from the starlight
burns up the lands hostile
to poor working people.
Mildness in us slaves is fear:
we're only after the esteem
of the bosses, for which the first
christian virtue of our nature
is allowed to offend and oppress us.

I who was humble, my son,
have given you the love of power.
The honey born from the onion
tempts the fledgling children,
the last born to our misery.
Humility in us slaves is respect

for the will of the owner:
Whatever he is seems extraordinary
to one who only owns a naked
lumpen proletarian heart in his chest.

Son, I who was honest
have given you a love of betrayal.
The wind born from the little cloud
invisibly attacks the forest
carrying death and subversion.
Honesty for slaves is a struggle
with themselves to keep from the gallows.
Praise for their good behavior
is the blessing of a corrupt hand
amid the heavenly smoke of the censer.

I who was only life, my son,
have given you the love of death.
Fate, born from prehistory,
upsets history's coming to pass,
through the fury of the insurgent masses.
Because the simple life of us slaves
is a force that in itself holds no dominion:
fountain of unforeseeable destinies,
you've sucked the milk of heroism
and of murderers from my breast.

My son, how many mothers in the world
are still making sons like you,
in Asia, Europe, Africa, where
lands of slaves, bandits, and thieves are

"dreaming of something" deep inside.
Mothers in whom sin is innocence,
mildness rancor, power humility,
honesty betrayal: and whose life bestows
a thirst for death: it needs knowledge,
conscience or piety isn't enough.

1961–62. Translated by Jack Hirschman

THE PCI[1] TO YOUNG PEOPLE!

It's sad. The polemic against
the Italian CP was to be done
in the first half
of the past decade. You're late, sons!
And it doesn't matter if you weren't even born then . . .
Now journalists from all over the world
(including television ones)
lick (as I believe that's still used in University
language) your ass. I don't, friends!
You have spoiled rich young men's faces.
Good breeding doesn't lie.
You have the same mean look.
You're fearful, uncertain, desperate
(alright) but you can also be
bullies, blackmailers, and cocksure:
petty-bourgeois prerogatives, friends.
When yesterday at Valle Giulia[2] you came to blows
with the cops, I was on their side!
Because the cops are sons of poor people.
They come from the outskirts, whether rural or urban.
As for me, I know very well
the way they were as children and young boys,
the precious *thousand-lire*, the father no more than a boy too
because of poverty, that confers no authority.
The mother callous as a drudge, or tender,

---

1. The Italian Communist Party.
2. Area in Rome where fights between students and cops occurred.

because of some illness, like a little bird;
the many brothers, the hovel
among fields with red sage (on others'
land, parcelled out); the lower floors
over the sewers; or the flats in the huge
common blocks, etc., etc.
And then, look how they're dressed up: like clowns,
with that coarse fabric stinking of mess rations
and the common people. Worse than everything, of course,
is the psychological state they're reduced to
(for barely forty thousand lire a month):
with no longer a smile,
no longer in friendship with the world,
separated,
excluded (in an exclusion that has no equal);
humiliated by the loss of their quality as human beings
for that of the cops (to be hated leads to hate).
They're twenty, they're as old as you, dear boys and girls.
Obviously we're against the institution of police.
But blame the judiciary and you'll see what happens!
The young cops
that you, in the holy vandalism (from the chosen tradition
of the Renaissance)
of spoiled rich young men, beat up
belong to the other social class.
At Valle Giulia, yesterday, there was indeed a fragment
of class struggle: and you, friends (though on the right
side) were the rich,
while the cops (who were on the wrong
side) were the poor. Nice victory, indeed,
yours! In cases like these

the cops get the flowers, friends.
Popolo and *Corriere della Sera, Newsweek,* and *Monde*
lick your ass. You're their sons,
their hope, their future: if they reproach you,
no way are they getting ready for a class struggle
against you! If anything, it's
for the old internecine struggle.
For whoever, intellectual or worker,
is outside your struggle, it's very funny the idea
that a young bourgeois gives an old bourgeois
a good thrashing, and that an old bourgeois sends a young
        bourgeois
to jail. Blandly
Hitler times are returning: the bourgeoisie
loves punishing itself with its own hands.
I apologize to those one or two thousands young brothers of
        mine
who are active in Trento or Torino,
Pavia or Pisa,
Florence, and a little in Roma also,
but I have to say: the Student Protest Movement
doesn't deal with the gospels, whose reading
its middle-aged flatterers credit it with,
to feel young and create blackmailing virginities for
        themselves:
students really know only one thing:
the moralism of their magistrate or white-collar fathers,
the conformist violence of their elder brothers
(of course in the fathers' footsteps)
the hatred their mothers, of peasant origins,
even if now remote in time, have for culture.

You know this, dear sons.
And you apply it through two inescapable feelings:
Consciousness of your rights (it's well known, democracy
considers only you) and the striving
for power.
Yes, your slogans are always about
the taking of power.
I read in your beards impotent ambitions;
in your paleness, desperate snobbisms;
in your shifty eyes, sexual dissociations;
in your iron health, arrogance; in your bad health, scorn
(only in the few of you who come from the lowest
bourgeoisie, or from some working family,
do these defects have some nobility:
know thyself, and Barbiana's school!).[3]
You occupy the universities
but you say that the young workers
have the same idea.
And so:
will *Corriere della Sera* and *Popolo*, *Newsweek* and *Monde*
be so solicitous in
attempting to comprehend their troubles?
Will the cops limit themselves by taking a little beating
in an occupied factory?
It's a banal observation;
it's blackmailing. But mainly it's vain:
because you're bourgeois,
that is, anti-communists. The workers, they're

---

3. A radical school created by Don Milani in the '50s to help fringe and marginal-
ized kids.

still in 1950 and even further back.
An idea as ancient as Resistance (which had to be contested
twenty years ago—
and the worse for you if you weren't born yet)
still takes root in people's breasts in the suburbs.
It may be that the workers speak neither French nor English,
and there's only some poor guy at night, in a Party room,
trying hard to learn some Russian.
Stop thinking of your rights,
stop asking for power.
A redeemed bourgeois must renounce all his rights
and banish from his soul, once and for all,
the idea of power. All that is liberalism: leave it
to Bobby Kennedy.
Masters make themselves by occupying factories
not universities: your flatterers (communists also)
never tell you the banal truth, that you're a new
idealist species of anythingarians like your fathers were,
and still are, sons.
Well,
the Americans, your adorable peers,
with their foolish flowers, are inventing
a "new" revolutionary language!
They're inventing it day by day!
But you can't do the same because in Europe there's already
          one:
could you be unaware of it?
Yes, you want to be unaware of it (to the great satisfaction
of the *Times* and *Tempo*).
You ignore it, going, with deep provincial moralism,
"more and more to the Left." It's strange:

giving up the revolutionary language of
the poor, old, *togliattiesque,*[4] official
Communist Party,
you adopted a heretical variant of it
but on the basis of the lowest jargon
of sociologists with no ideology (or of dumb bureaucrats).
Speaking this way,
you claim everything with words,
while, with facts,
you claim only what
you have the right to (as good bourgeois sons):
a series of urgent reforms,
the application of new pedagogic methods
and the renewal of a State system.
Nice ones! Sacred sentiments!
May the lucky star of the bourgeoisie assist you!
Inebriated by your victory over young
cops obliged to be servants by poverty,
(and drunk on the interest of bourgeois
public opinion with which you behave like women
not in love, who ignore and mistreat
the rich wooer),
you put aside the only truly dangerous instrument
to fight against your fathers:
that is, communism.
I hope you've understood
    that pretending Puritanism
    is a way to prevent oneself from

---

4. An adjective made from the name of Palmiro Togliatti, 1893–1964, the leader of
the Italian Communist Party (PCI) from 1927 till his death.

a truly revolutionary action.
But instead, sonnies, go and assault the Federations!
Go and invade the Party cells!
Go and occupy the Central Committee offices! Go, go
and camp out in *Via delle Botteghe Oscure*!
If you want power, at least seize the power
of a Party that's nevertheless of the opposition
(even if it's in bad shape because of the authority of
        gentlemen
in modest double-breasted coats, bocce-ball enthusiasts, lovers
        of understatement,
bourgeois peers of your foolish fathers),
and has as its theoretical goal the destruction of Power.
In the meantime I very much doubt that it'll decide
to destroy what of the bourgeoisie it has in itself,
even with your contribution, if, as I said,
good breeding doesn't lie . . .
Anyway: the PCI to young people!

But, now, what am I suggesting to you? What am I
advising? What am I
urging you to do?
I repent, I repent
I took the path leading to the lesser evil,
may God damn me. Don't listen to me!
Oh, oh, oh
the blackmailer's blackmailed,
I was sounding the trumpets of good sense!
I stopped just in time,
saving both
fanatic dualism and ambiguity . . .

But I've arrived at the fringes
of shame . . .
(oh God! Do I have to take into consideration
the possibility of fighting the Civil War on your side,
setting aside my old idea of Revolution?)

1968. Translated by Giada Diano

APOLOGY

What are "bad verses" (as presumably these, "The PCI to Young People," are)? It's very simple: bad verses are those that on their own can't express what the author wants to: that is, in them, meanings are distorted by connotations and, at the same time, connotations obfuscate meanings.

Poetry, we know, gets its signs from different semantic fields, fitting them together, often arbitrarily; then it makes each sign a sort of stratification in which every layer corresponds to a sign's meaning, derived from a different semantic field but temporarily fitting in with the others (by means of a demon).

Therefore: yes, bad verses are comprehensible, but good will is needed to comprehend them.

I doubt the good will of many of the readers of these bad verses: also because, in many cases, I'll have to expect from them, so to speak, "a bad will in good faith." That is, a political passion as valid as mine, which, as mine, has got hopes and bitterness, idols and hatreds.

Let it be clear that I wrote these bad verses in several registers at the same time: so they're all "split in two," that is, ironic and self-ironic. Everything is said in quotes. The piece on the cops is a piece of rhetorical art that a mad Bolognese lawyer could define, as the case in point, as a "captatio malevolentiae" (a malevolent grab): therefore the quotes are those of provocation. I hope my good reader's bad will "accepts" the provocation, since it's a provocation on a sympathetic level. (Those that can't be accepted are the provocations of fascists and the police.) In quotes, for example, are also the two pieces concerning the old workers going to the Party room by night to learn Russian, and the evolution of the good old, broken-down PCI—besides the fact that objectively such worker and PCI figures correspond also to "reality"; here in this poem, they're rhetorical and paradoxical figures, still provocative.

The only non-provocative piece, even if said in a fatuous tone, is the parenthetical and final one. Here I do raise, although from behind an ironic and bitter screen (I couldn't suddenly convert the demon that frequented me, immediately after the Valle Giulia fight, and I insist upon chronology also for the ones who are not philologists), a "real" question. There's this dilemma in the future: civil war or revolution?

I can't act as many of my friends, who pretend to confuse the two things (or they truly do it!), and caught up in the "student psychosis" fling themselves on the students' side (flattering the students and receiving contempt); neither can I state that every revolutionary possibility is ruined, and that we have to opt (as, in a different historical destiny, is happening in America or in Bonn's Germany) for "civil war": in fact, as I said many times, the bourgeoisie is fighting the civil war against itself. Nor, finally, am I so cynical (like French people) as to think that we could make the revolution "profit" from the civil war unleashed by the students—and discard them afterward, even perhaps bump them off.

These bad verses came into being from this state of mind and their dominant characteristic is, anyway, provocation (and they express it indiscriminately, because of their ugliness). But, and this is the point, why have I challenged the students so much (so that some greasy private newspaper could even speculate on it)?

This is the reason why: until my own generation, young people had the bourgeoisie in front of them as an "object," a "separated" world (separated from them because, of course, I'm speaking of excluded young people, excluded because of a trauma—and let's take as trauma the typical one of 19-year-old Lenin, who saw his brother hanged by the police). Therefore we could look at the bourgeoisie, objectively, from the outside (even if we were awfully implicated with it through history, school, church, anguish): we were offered a way to look objectively at the bourgeoisie, according to a typical pattern, by looking at it from what was not bourgeois: workers or peasants (from what, later on, would be called the Third World). Therefore we, young intellectuals of 20 or 30 years ago (and, by class privilege, students) could be anti-bourgeois outside of the bourgeoisie as well, through the perspective offered us by the other social classes (revolutionary, or rebellious as they were).

We grew up, therefore, with the idea of the revolution in our mind: of the workers' and peasants' revolution (Russia '17, China, Cuba, Algeria, Vietnam). Consequently we made traumatic hatred of the bourgeoisie a just perspective, wherein to integrate our actions, in a non-evasive future (at least partially, because we're all a little sentimental).

For young people today things are different: for them it's much more difficult to look objectively at the bourgeoisie through another social class's gaze. Because the bourgeoisie is triumphing, it's making the workers bourgeois, on one side, and the peasants ex-colonials on the other. In brief, through neo-capitalism, the bourgeoisie is becoming the human condition. Whoever was born into this entropy can't be, metaphysically, outside it. It's over. That's why I provoke young people: they presumably are the last generation to see workers and peasants: the next generation will only see bourgeois entropy around itself.

Now, I am, personally (my private exclusion much more atrocious than the one affecting, for example, a Black or a Jew, as a young boy) and publicly (fascism and war, with which I've opened my eyes to life—how many hangings! how many deaths on hooks!) so traumatized by the bourgeoisie that my hatred against it is pathological by now. I can expect nothing from it, neither as a totality, nor as creator of antibodies against itself (as happens in entropies: the antibodies growing up in the American entropy exist, and have a reason to, only because there are negroes in America: for a young American boy, they have the same function that workers and poor peasants had for us when young).

Given this "total" distrust I have of the bourgeoisie, I resist, indeed, the idea of a civil war, where perhaps, through the students' explosion, the bourgeoisie would fight against itself. I'd say young people of this generation already are physically much more bourgeois than us. So then? Don't I have the right to provoke them? How else could I have a relation with them, if not in this way? The demon who tempted me is a demon, as is known, full of vices: this time it also had the vice of impatience and lovelessness toward that old craftsmanship that art is: I've made a single untidy bundle of all the semantic fields, regretting even not being very pragmatic, that is, embracing as well the semantic fields that carry non-linguistic communications, i.e., physical presence and action. . . . To conclude, then, today young students belong to a "totality" (the "semantic fields" they express themselves with, through both linguistic and non-linguistic communication); they're closely unified and fenced off, consequently they're unable, I believe, to understand on their own that when they define themselves as "petty-bourgeois" in their self-criticisms, they make an elementary and unconscious mistake: in fact today the petty-bourgeois no longer has peasant grandparents but great-grandparents and maybe great-great-grandparents; he hasn't lived an anti-bourgeois revolutionary (worker) experience pragmatically (hence the pointless fumbling around looking for worker comrades); on the contrary he's experienced the first type of neo-capitalism's quality of life, with the problems of total industrialization. Today the petty-bourgeois is, therefore, no longer the one defined in Marxism's classics, for example, in Lenin. (As, for example, today China is no longer Lenin's China: and therefore, to quote the example of "China" from Lenin's booklet on imperialism would be madness.) Moreover, today young people (and may they hurry up, abandon the horrendous classist denomination of students, and become young intellectuals) don't realize how revolting a petty-bourgeois of today is, and that both the workers (in spite of the persistent optimism of communist canon) and the poor peasants (in spite of their mythification operated upon by intellectuals following Marcuse and Fanon—myself too, but ante-litteram) are conforming themselves to such a model.

Therefore students can arrive at this Manichaean consciousness of bourgeois evil (to sum up):

a) by re-analyzing—outside of sociology as well as of Marxism's classics—the petty-bourgeois they are (we are) today;

b) by abandoning their own ontological and tautological self-definition of "students" and accepting being simply some "intellectuals";

c) by working on the last still-possible choice—on the eve of the identification of bourgeois history with human history—in favor of what is not bourgeois (something they can do now only by substituting the force of reason with the public and private traumatic reasons I was hinting at before—an extremely difficult operation, implying an "ingenious" self-analysis, outside of every orthodoxy).

1968. Translated by Giada Diano

THE WORKER'S COUGH

I hear the worker coughing down below;
his cough comes up through the ground-floor grating
giving onto my garden, so that it avoids resonating among the
    plants
touched by the sun on this last morning of good weather. He,
the worker, down below, intent at his job, coughs now and then
pretty sure no one's hearing it. It's a seasonal sickness
but his cough's not a good one; it's worse than a flu.
He endures the illness, takes care of it, I imagine, like we
did when we were kids. Life for him remains decidedly un-
    comfortable;
no rest awaits him at home after work,
exactly like it is with us poor or almost poor guys.
See, life seemed to us to consist entirely of that poverty
in which one doesn't even have the right—naturally—
to the quiet use of a john or the solitude of a bed;
and when illness comes it's received heroically:
a worker's always 18, even if he has kids
bigger than him, ones new to those heroisms.
In short, in those wracking coughs
the tragic meaning of this beautiful October sun is revealed.

                    1969. Translated by Jack Hirschman

CIVIL CANTO

Their cheeks were fresh and tender
and kissed maybe for the first time.
Seen from behind, when they turned
to return to the gentle group, they were more adult,
with overcoats over light trousers. Their poverty
forgets it's a cold winter. Their legs a little bowed
with collars frayed like their older brothers',
already discredited citizens. Still, for some years
they're priceless: and there can't be anything humiliating
in one who can't be judged. For, since they do it
with so much incredible naturalness, offering themselves to
    life,
life asks for them. They're so ready for it!
They give back kisses, testing the novelty.
Then they leave as undisturbed as they came.
But since they're still full of trusting that life loves them,
they make sincere promises, project a promising future
of hugs, and kisses as well. Who could make the revolution
—if ever one needed to make it—if not them? Tell them so:
    they're ready,
all in the same way, just as they hug and kiss
with the same smell on their cheeks.
But it won't be their trust in the world that will triumph.
That's what the world must ignore.

              1969. Translated by Jack Hirschman

LINES OF A TESTAMENT

One needs to be very strong
to love solitude; one needs to have good legs
and an unusual resistance; one shouldn't risk
catching a cold, or flu or a sore throat; you mustn't
be afraid of robbers and killers; if one has to walk
through an afternoon or even all night long
one needs to know how to do it without even thinking.
There's no chance for one to sit, particularly
in winter; with a wind that blows over the wet grass
and with big, wet, muddy stones between garbage,
there's really no relief—no doubt about it—
beyond that of having a whole day and night ahead of one
without duties or limits of whatever kind.
Sex is a pretext. Because the encounters are many
—in winter too, on streets abandoned to the wind,
among the litter strewn against the distant buildings—
they're many—but they're only moments of loneliness;
the warmer and more alive the gentle body is
that anoints with sperm and moves on,
the colder and more mortal the beloved desert is around one;
and that's what fills one with joy,
like a miraculous wind, not the innocent smile
or the gloomy insolence of the one who goes away;
he carries with him a youth that's enormously young
and in this he's inhuman
because he leaves no traces, or rather he leaves
a single trace that's always
the same one in every season.

A young man in his first loves
is nothing else but the fecundity of the world.
It's the world that arrives with him: he appears and disappears
like changing form. All things remain intact
and you could walk half the city and not find him again.
The act's done, its repetition's a ritual. So
loneliness is even greater if a whole crowd
waits its turn: the number of disappearances in fact grows—
going away is fleeing—and
what follows looms over the present
like a duty, a sacrifice to offer to death's desire.
In getting older, however, weariness begins to be felt,
particularly in the moment just after dinnertime,
when for you nothing's changed; then, for a hair's breath,
you don't cry out or weep;
and that would be enormous if it weren't just the weariness
and maybe a bit of hunger. Enormous because
it'd mean that your desire for solitude
couldn't ever be satisfied, and so isn't what's
awaiting you, if not considered solitude,
real solitude, what you can't accept?
There's no dinner or lunch or satisfaction
in the world that's worth an endless stroll
through poor streets where one needs to be
wretched and strong, brothers of dogs.

1971. Translated by Jack Hirschman

FORTINI'S OBSESSIONS

A book of old poems by Franco Fortini, *Poesia e Errore* (Mondadori), has just come out. I say old because it had been written and published between 1946 and 1957.

This isn't a review of the book but an opportunity for a marginal note. In fact I'd have very little to say about the book: what interests me for this note instead is a booklet or excerpt that's inserted as a body apart within the pages of the volume. It's a group of 25 recent poems, written from 1961 to 1968. These poems don't represent anything new stylistically compared with the rest of the work. They're configured as well as a "fleeing from zeal"—a second thought from a pathetic zone—with metaphysical and crepuscular traits, that remind one a little bit of Luzi[1]—about subjects discussed somewhere else and with much more vigor, necessity, and geniality by the author, in his capacity as essayist and moralist, that is, as a man of politics. What's really curious about these poems, what concerns my actual interest in the political situation, are the stylistic references, at a level a little ingenuously metaphorical, to the terminological world of war. In these same columns I've already talked about the illusions, on the part of some leaders of political youth movements, of a waged war partly going on, partly imminent, for which we should in any case prepare, considering ourselves in a state of emergency. And I was being a little ironic (bitterly, of course) about this zeal whose awkwardness is unfolded in a way that's very schematic, rough, brutal, and even a little demagogic: the war is waged by the workers and only the Italian Communist

---

1. Mario Luzi (1914–2006), renowned poet.

Party can conduct it. A war waged by young intellectuals, con-
ducted by the student movement or by the *Quaderni Piacentini*[2]
isn't thinkable, and it even opens itself up to being the target of
ironic attacks (which I feel ashamed of but which something
turbid, bitter, and unjust pushes me to do).

Fortini's poems (old or recent) are a confirmation of the
raison d'être of this sad irony of mine. All of Fortini's poems
seem to have been written during a "pause from the fight"
(something that after all corresponds to reality). At nightfall,
when the gunfire eases off, the warriors make a fire, some
start to sing, some play the guitar, some write letters home,
and someone curled up in a dark corner, which the moon can
hardly reach, writes his beloved verses in a small notebook.
But it's clear anyway that for Fortini the metahistoricism of the
poetic act (that occurs necessarily during a "pause," in a corner
outside action, in a secret fold of history) counts because it's
still a second thought of the fight, through a simple change of
register. I'm going to make here a quick list of the *war refer-
ences* in Fortini's poems. The second poem is titled "The Light
of Fire" and it starts with: "the trenches were here"; and it ends
like this: "with haste and pity, we took turns; in a while there'll
be the assault." The third poem is titled "Speech of the Gov-
ernor" and it ends with this verse: "Don't look at those fires
up on the mountain" (fires of a mysterious army). The fourth
poem is titled "After a Massacre." Here is a fragment of it: "On
the wall they have changed the great imperial flags—Lives of
friends become ghosts, I can't bear to look at them.—In anger
against bushes of swords I look for a little poem.—No com-
plaining. I bow my head. It's no longer possible to write." In

---

2. An important cultural and political journal.

"The Difficulties of the Paint Factory": "We'd be happy if we had only enemies up front." In "From the Hill" (a hill between a Montalian[3] one and a Partisan one): "Tell how they've killed us, and the names of our enemies." From "Advices": "Don't separate from my pronunciation, the deaf sounds and the clear ones; because of friends and necessary enemies, they'll always have news for you." From "Saint Miniato": "If the dead could see, they'd see like me.—They'd hear this cry of people killed by. . . ." Anyway, in all the poems, the element that up until a year ago was called obligatorily "structural" is the allusion to the fight and the right to pause while fighting, which occur always in a place in the country or on hills: a) similar to places of Partisan battles, b) linked by mysterious analogies to the rural world of the Chinese Cultural Revolution. Even the three funeral remembrances (Elio Vittorini,[4] Raniero Panzieri,[5] and his own father) recall the poetic gravestones for the fallen.

It's an obsession with waging war: that reflects, against a necessarily ambiguous poetic screen, the idea that Fortini currently has of *situation* as a situation of emergency in which the poet should transform himself into a strategist, a soldier. If Fortini's idea of the situation were correct and corresponded to reality, his metaphors would have meaning; if on the other hand his idea were arbitrary and illusory, then those metaphors would have a whole other meaning. I believe in this second hypothesis. But Fortini, I think, needs to feel himself in a war, because only in this way can he exist and find necessity to his existence. Peace (the "religion of everyday life") is something that fate hadn't

---

3. Adjective formed from the name of Eugenio Montale, Italy's foremost poet of the '50s and '60s.

4. Vittorini (1908-1966), important novelist.

5. Socialist Party writer and translator of Marx.

planned for him—it only interests him as a nostalgia that gnaws during the truce in fighting. As a Jew by necessity and as a man of politics by choice, Fortini never had the right to peace. And this makes him a brother and dear to me. But his blindness in facing reality, and the fanaticism that's bound to derive from reality, pushes me to argue with him. We're in a war. The working class and the Italian Communist Party don't want this war. What the Student Movement has is an illusion of war. Therefore Fortini moves, thinks, and acts outside reality, like a poet. . . . Nevertheless, being a poet is for him a cause of shame: among his rigid comrades he has to find an excuse, he has to try a sort of continuous pathetic "captatio benevolentiae" according to which the sole valuable category for judging a man is utility.

The idea of war to which Fortini makes continuous references, isn't the real war (which in reality isn't fought), but a purely metaphorical one, curiously archaic. It reminds one of the poor Partisan war[6] or even the 1915–1918 war, with its trenches, its gunshots, its goodbyes, etc. Such metaphorical war is therefore like a form of imagination, an archaic form, and *therefore it represents a belated content.* Everyone can see here the incurable contradiction in the depth of the revolutionary Fortini. After all he's aware of it, and this is quite clear in the sense of the linguistic decency that he feels when he makes "the cry to the poet," to the poet alone within himself, wholly intent on his old contemplations about "his" nature—with the eternal leaves, the forests, the seasons. Here Fortini's biggest concern seems to be that of stylizing and making comprehensible (and forgivable) the grazing and awful desperation of the ascent that's fundamentally based

---

6. The war waged by the Italian Partisans against the fascists during the Second World War.

on nothingness, though a sort of codification capable of being deciphered by everyone: a Leopardian,[7] Montalian nothingness laid bare by the marvelous indifference of nature and by man as a being. This is something that Fortini tends in vain to mask by trying to transform even this circumstance into a lesson (his forefathers speak within him with a raised finger), or tries to mask by looking for the complicity of the reader as a comrade. What comes out of this is a poetry that is "used up," that relives, in falsetto, the emotions of the serious poets (the fathers): the poetic Italian of Fortini is similar to that of Bassani.[8] A modest "melody": whose result is perfectly manneristic. Fortini's in the grip of a dilemma as well: he cheats, pretending to be outside of it, in a different "tension." Those who are forced every day to bear being thrashed at the degrading level of television and consumerism are not the only ones in the scheme: *he's in it too* (even if atheist, poetic), raised up in a zealous pact with action.

As for me, when earlier I bitterly said that the working class and the Italian Communist Party don't want the war, I was saying that by assuming an attitude ingloriously neutral and "realistic." And when I said that the Student Movement couldn't wage the war, I wanted to say that armies wage war and armies are *institutions*.

1969. Translated by Veruska Cantelli

---

7. Adjective formed from the name of Giacomo Leopardi, the most renowned Italian poet of the 19th century.

8. Giorgio Bassani (1916–2000), poet and friend of Pasolini.

OSIP MANDELSTAM

I have in my hands a small book of poetry by Osip Mandelstam and beside it, the big volume of memories by his wife, the heroic, the staunch Nadezhda Mandelstam. I also see, grainy and blurry, the photo of Mandelstam as a boy, a nice-looking Jewish boy, sensual and intelligent. I'm in the state of mind of someone who has to give a funeral eulogy, or to write some "civic" verse, like they did in the '50s, about something whose significance, which rips through the story like a hurt destined to be an incurable wound, is so decidedly tragic as to end up almost luminous and marvelous.

Was it a life, that life of Mandelstam? I don't think it resembles any I've known or felt or imagined. It doesn't hark back to "human tradition" which sees the lives of one's fellows as very similar, one to another, or as very varied, but of a piece. Mandelstam lived like a man in strange pastures. To those around him, maybe he seemed like everyone else, just trying to live. For this we have the testimony, minute and unending, of his wife . . . yes, Mandelstam did live in the material sense: he gave the impression of a person living a life like everyone else does; he expressed ideas, literary ideas, had political opinions, and acted accordingly. And yet his life followed certain stages, had its rhythms, and what was set in motion by these things wasn't recognizable as life, more like a wretched brawl, eternally infantile. Every once in a while he seemed to have finally matured; at these points he would cheer up, have a pause of tender and spirited happiness. At the same time never, as in these moments, did his life seem so sadly lacking, negated, hopeless.

Maybe there was a mistake at the outset. A banal error.

When he was 20, he shouldn't have gone to the university at St. Petersburg. He'd have done better at Heidelberg or Paris. Of course, if he was really going to be part of the Russian literary scene, he'd have had to go to St. Petersburg, but even then the idea should have been to return to the West. He was a Jew. He had nothing to lose. He couldn't become stateless. He would have had a real life, which is just what it was, up to now; the youth of a young Polish Jewish bourgeois who is leaving his native Warsaw in search of intelligence, culture, and a future.

But he stayed in St. Petersburg. Why? Here begins the absurdity of his life, which is unlike anyone else's absurdity, because *absurd* doesn't quite explain it. It was in fact reasonable and honorable to stay in St. Petersburg, to live the revolution, to take part, even if only as a poet, in the grand historical social changes of that era, a poet who "feels in debt to the revolution compared to what it has given him, but who brings it gifts it can't use right now." So it was only fair and right that he should try to find a place in it, to get involved in this new world that the revolution brought forth. But as early as 1923 he got his first official "invitation" to not publish any more verses! In advance yet. Since he didn't have a lot of nerve and didn't know how to react in any way (at least that's how it looks) Mandelstam didn't react. His defense was: playing dead, accepting everything, not accusing anyone. But even this is just and reasonable if you figure that, at the same time, with his own crazy way of being lucid and stubborn, Mandelstam did start an opposition, isolated and inward, that could have led him to a "Hero's Death." This contradiction between such a revolutionary opposition to the revolution and his continual, futile, self-deluding attempts to pretend that everything was O.K., to appease the evil one, to bend to him, was also explainable; it's a normal element of human life.

We recognize it. Even so, up to his arrest in '34 right in the middle of the Stalin era, the life of Mandelstam continued to run a unique course, which was modeled maybe more on the dreams and books of Kafka than on anything we're familiar with. But the alienation of Kafka was the kind you see under capitalism, whereas Mandelstam's alienation had a less recognizable, less normal form, estranged as he was, remaining a child and impotent in a Communist world.

What is tragic, more than his bitter, prudently enacted battle with Stalin, was his search for contentment, his pathetic efforts at appeasement, his menial editorial jobs, his voyages, and his routines, all of which seeming to make him happy enough in whatever small, quiet apartment in Moscow he was in. And all this meniality from a privileged guy, destined for wealth, and more or less at home in the culture of the rich. Teetering on a branch of life, which was, at that time, the non-life of those who accepted Stalin's dictatorship, Mandelstam thus lived a life of unreality, for which *there was no solution*. Maybe he would have had one authentic feeling: to escape. Or maybe not. We have no way of knowing. What we see him really working hard at is going from the frying pan into the fire and, as for the reasons he had, we have only the testimony of his scant verses.

So it was that he went along and dissolved into the void. His death was announced by "official notices" that claimed him dead at the transit camp Vtoraja Recka, near Vladivostok. Before that he had been in a compulsory residence at Cerdyn (where he had tried suicide), and afterwards a stop at the compulsory dorm of Voronez; then in '38 he was officially arrested and deported. (Today in the U.S.S.R. his works are still only read clandestinely.)

Quick, intelligent, spirited, elegant, or better yet exquisite, gay, sensual; always in love, loyal, lucid, and happy right in the middle of his neuroses and the political horror show; juvenile, in fact almost like a boy, whimsical and cultured; faithful and inventive, smiling and patient, Mandelstam has given us some of the happiest poetry of the century, much happier than that of Mayakovsky and richer, even if in a more narrow frame of reference, than that of Esenin.

Mandelstam was, at this time, part of the movement in Russian culture called formalism, even if you have to stretch the historical time limits of the period to fit him in. He didn't, in fact, participate directly in this movement and he didn't really get into the meta-linguistical aspect of formalism; he applied himself to the problem of the language of poetry but he found his answers without leaving the language of poetry. There's one field of interest for him other than this: Politics lived as life. It is ridiculous to have him pass for a champion of the "independence of art"! In the field of formal research he had all the elements of formalism, but he had them in original styles, in a moment of purity not yet codified in poetic or literary manifestos; in this way the "writing style" of formalism, light, fatuous and profound, breezy and absolute, full of cheap and chaste puns, mixed in him with the "writing style" of a precedent or better yet just-short-of-contemporary European literary culture—I would say paradoxically more like Apollinaire and Cocteau than Yeats and Eliot, for example. Not only that: in Mandelstam you have mixed together two loves, that of surrealism and its Russian version, "cubo-futurism," with that of symbolism: how often the "lightness" of Mandelstam ended up being expressed in the "hard rock" of an idiom mythically classical!

There is no real evolution in the poetry of Mandelstam; it's all of a piece. Perhaps only in some of his last verses, especially among the very last written at Voronez in '37, might you have a larger abstraction, and his material for inspiration, the countryside, the quality of the life that surrounds him, is at this point more mute and grey. No longer in Mandelstam is the affectionate spirit that sought out domestic and slightly silly details of everyday life, the "things" seen by an eye that enjoyed them from the privileged position of poet and potential bourgeois, in the most noble and respectful sense of the word. What was around him at Voronez was not for him, and the joy, the spirit, the humor that never left him could only be exercised in the world of himself, thus allowing him, walking a tightrope of linguistics, to deal with a tragic situation, certainly not of that world around him.

Mandelstam's creativity remained, even in the course of an unrealized life in a culture that couldn't adapt to its new challenges. To survive, he evidently always had to run back to the beginning, to drink at the primal fountains of himself.

And so there's not a verse or a couplet in any of this poetry that doesn't represent, as if solid, the spirit of Mandelstam: It's almost always a question of a verse playing between light flippancy and an analogous linguistic approach; thus we have the delightful scandal of the word-plays and the stupor of the formal, serving to light the spark of that dreamlike wisdom that understands and deals with all the world as if it were a secret and radiant novelty; this approach being either acquired by Mandelstam or possessed by him as an expressive talent, all his life. ". . . I envy all in secret, and with all in secret I'm in love"; "The senses are vanity, the word nothing more than noise / when the phonetic is in the service of the seraph"; "In fury of frivolity we are losing our minds"; "By the blessed word without meaning / I will pray to the soviet night"; "With the world of power I have nothing but puerile relations"; "Because in my veins there is not wolf's blood / there is only one of my peers who can slay me"; "And just who is it who's the real juvenile among us?"; "I desire to leave our language / and even so I'll always be its debtor"; "Dio-Nachtigal, give me the destiny of Pilade / or cut out my tongue"; "Power is repugnant like the hands of a barber"; "Don't make comparisons: a living one is incomparable"; "Everyone wants to see everything, / the born, the ones driven to ruin, the ones who refuse to die" etc., etc. All the "savvy" of Mandelstam is thus articulated, producing four or five of the most beautiful poems of the century, full of love, empty of love, full of hate, free of hatred: a battle against "not-being" fought in the catatonia of a dream in which the conscience, though it may well be impotent, can very well be lucid and almost, mysteriously, happy.

1972. Translated by Jonathan Richman

ITALO CALVINO'S *INVISIBLE CITIES*

I grew up with Italo Calvino; I saw him when very young, almost a boy (I believe he is one or two years younger than I am, but when I entered the world coming out from what I call the Friuli monastery in 1950, he was a bit more of an adult, and he was more inside the things of society and of literature, which were off limits for me for a bit longer, almost as if I did not deserve them, for some indignity—or for too much ingenuity). We worked together, Calvino in Torino, myself in Rome, up until we were 40 years old, meaning up until the moment we reached the center of life (40 years is the age when a man is more "deluded," he believes more in the so-called world values, he takes more seriously the idea that he has to participate in it, that he has to take them over. The 20-year-old, compared to a 40-year-old, is a monster of realism). Our work somehow integrated itself, even if it was so different: and what linked us was an optimism—like a good feeling—that consisted of the conviction that our work was at the "center" of something, and that something should result from it. In a shadowy way, we admired and loved each other, without too many compliments; we were too involved in the importance of what we were doing to allow disinterested pauses.

Then Calvino stopped feeling close to me. I understood that right away. At the beginning of the Sixties, something was cracking, and he and I were on the two opposite sides of the crack. His military face, smart and proud, underneath the big black eyebrows that, even if he is so northern, made him so Mediterranean, the full lips that are always agitated just as if he's about to say something that's cheerfully passing by in his

116

attentive brain—this image of his already started to fade away and lose its colors, to smile from far away, like one of a dear person whose loss is known after a few years, when it's too late to suffer about it. Of course I've something to say against the way Calvino chose "current events": his opening towards the neo-avant-garde and his aprioristic attachment to the Student Movement (just to remain on a more general ground). I don't know what happened *really* in his head in these last years, because Calvino, maybe diplomatically, didn't speak, or he lied a little bit. Something that, after all, one has to know how to do in this world. Who says that one should always say the truth? Sometimes it's better to avoid speaking than to tell the truth. Sometimes it's healthier to keep the truth inside oneself. At any rate Calvino maintained his credit intact, while I was discredited twice, by two fashions from which on the other hand Calvino didn't dissociate himself—establishing with them a sort of distracted alliance—with the re-establishment of the truth that I, inopportunely, screamed left and right like a plucked hen—I continue to enjoy not only the discredit (which reveals itself as quite undeserved), but also the antipathy of people who can't forgive me for having said back then what it was right to say. As I was saying I didn't hear anything about Calvino for a few years, almost as if also physically he had a sort of suspension. The *Cosmos Comix*—I confess it—arrived as something unreal and interlocutory. Now he reappears to me not only real, but realer than ever, with his last book, which not only is his most beautiful, but also is beautiful by definition.

The first observation I feel like making is that this book of his, *The Invisible Cities*, is the book of a boy. Only a boy can have on the one hand a humor so radiant, so pristine, so inclined to do beautiful things, resistant things, rejoicing things; and, on the other hand, only a boy can have so much patience—like an artisan who wants to finish and refinish his work at any cost. Not older people, it's the boys who are patient.

After all, in the city of Isidora, "there's the sitting place where older people watch youth go by; he's sitting among them." And without doubt, that is, following logic, *Invisible Cities* is the work of an old man, or at least of an older man, *who saw life passing by.* This experience—which is the most important that man can have—prevents him from seeing the future as the future of his own life, or even as the future of the sons or nephews (that is the human horizon within which, for example, Reason operates, and ethics, especially normative ethics, finds its own foundations): no, the experience of having seen life go by equals the experience of having seen *all* possible life, the life of the cosmos. Thus the future enlarges itself without limits, and all the proportions of the real, with its rationality and its morale, fall apart. What remains is the data of such an experience which, without rationality and without morals, has to justify itself since it can't confront itself with anything else but illusions and, on the other hand, has no other way out except that of expression.

Thus Calvino's book is a book of an old man, for whom "desires are memories." But not only are desires memories; notions also are memories, and information, the news, experiences, ideologies, logics—everything is memory. Every intellectual instrument to live is a memory.

Consequently, also, the absolute novelty of knowing life "as past" has no other instruments to express itself with but these old memories. Thus the truth is that each cultural illusion in Calvino has faded, but the culture has remained, at least as provider of those cultural memories, through which Calvino can express the new world as it presents itself to his old-boy dazzled eyes, sitting at the sitting place in his city of Isidora.

In this "survived" culture of Calvino, there is everything as well: of course, Marxism with its practical necessities of intervention, his rhetoric etc., because it's this above all that the book denies (but doesn't renounce) while incorporating it. The idea of a Better City, reached through victory, let's say, of the class struggle, is simply immersed in a different idea of time: I'm not saying of history, but precisely of time. In fact many cities dreamt by Calvino at some point reach perfection. The fact that they lose it again is something that concerns future generations. I say that in order to try to calm down the consciences of my observant Marxist colleague-critics.

So, in spite of the fall of every cultural illusion, Calvino's culture, I repeat, remained intact, even if only in the form of illusion: and, as such, it reached the formal perfection of an object, of a marvelous fossil. The specific culture of Calvino is the literary one, freed by its function, by its duties, and become like an abandoned mine where Calvino goes to withdraw whatever treasure he wants.

What does he withdraw? First of all, a metallic writing, almost pristine, but light, incredibly light: the writing of play. Calvino never transgresses this lightness: there's never a single instant in which he, while writing, doesn't go at full speed, as if he were going without an arrival point; but in this idea of going for the sake of going, the elegance, the disinterested care of elegance, is never betrayed, not even for a moment.

The second thing that Calvino withdraws from his unutilized cave are the techniques of ambiguity. On every page of *Invisible Cities* every canon is suspended, actually, is mocked. The feeling is like the one of an echo in a valley full of grottoes that resounds now here, now there, even if it's always the same sound.

But the ambiguity, in its most typical and classic aspect of infinite fading, can be found especially in the connective pages of the book, those in italics, which talk about the reports of a pseudo-Marco or of a pseudo-Polo to the emperor. Both interlocutors are eternally changing, and they present themselves, every time, as symbols of all potential books that this particular book could be; or like symbols of the points of view through which this book, both ideologically and linguistically, could be directed. Thus when we speak about Calvino, we can't speak about "relativism," because his relativism is totally visionary, faced with infinite different possibilities.

The third thing that Calvino takes out of his literary mine is surrealism: a surrealism that's a delight by definition, because you can't explain the gallery of surrealistic pictures that are a product of the writing, through themselves, meaning through surrealism. But the surrealistic pictures are functional in that crazy multiple ideology which argues against each potential reason, and most of all against the dialectical one.

The bottom line of such an infinitely possibilistic or multiple ideology is always the same, obsessively the same: it's constituted between the irreconcilable clash of two opposites: reality and the world of ideas. Yes, in Calvino's archaeological literature, Platonism, under whose sign that literature was born, pops up. All the cities that Calvino dreams about, in infinite forms, are born invariably from the clash between an ideal city and a real city: this clash has the effect of rendering surreal the real city, but isn't resolved in anything. The two opposites don't overcome each other in a dialectical relationship! The fight between them is as stubborn and desperate as it is useless: time brings peace, dragging everything with itself in a completely illogical dimension that solves problems by diluting them infinitely, destroying them until they're rotten and it's their turn to be surreal.

For me, since I am working on the film *A Thousand and One Nights*, reading this book has been almost intoxicating, and it's not by chance or based upon a personal interest. *A Thousand and One Nights* is precisely the figurative model that Calvino's surrealism sacks with parsimony, and like every tale from *A Thousand and One Nights*, it's the tale of an anomaly of destiny; also every description that Calvino makes is a description of an anomaly between the world of ideas and reality (which, after all, is Destiny in Western civilization). *Poetic invention consists of the individuation of that anomalous moment.*

In the descriptions of the cities Maurilia, Zobeide, Ipazia, Eutropia, Ottavia, Ersilia, Bauci, Pirra, Moriana, Bersabea, Raissa, Marozia, this individuation of anomaly is so perfect that it seemingly happened by itself: we have in front of us a phenomenon of a "surreal" reality of which Calvino seems to be the simple describer. How could something like that happen, when it's clear that, according to logic and practice, this operation in principle is extremely difficult if not impossible? How can one repeat the miracle of the narrator of *A Thousand and one Nights*, his exhilarating reliability in telling anomalies of the code of destiny? After all, this fact can be explained quite easily: rather, it's the first thing I should have said while talking about this book—Calvino doesn't invent anything just for the sake of invention. He simply concentrates on a real impression—one of the many intolerable shocks that afternoons or sunsets, middle seasons or hot days, cause in the most unthinkable or familiar corners of the known or unknown cities in which we live; and even if he feels his impression in all its tormented dreamy quality, he analyzes it: the separate pieces, taken apart in such analysis, are projected in the void and cosmic silence in which fantasy rebuilds dreams. It's always a "base" of real sensibility that gives materials for Calvino's poetic and ideological heights.

1973. Translated by Flavio Rizzo

MARY McCARTHY, *BIRDS OF AMERICA*

Not often does something happen like what happens when you read the book *Birds of America* by Mary McCarthy:[1] not often, that is to say, does this non-understanding of just what book you're reading occur. I should have kept a reader's diary in which to diligently write the progression of the things this book seemed to be or what I conjectured it wanted to be or, better still, the way in which I kept trying ways to categorize it, bit by bit, as I read.

Also, only rarely do we see a work so consistent, beginning to end, written with the same "hand," from first to last page, as if dictated by a will to not change style at all costs, to not deviate a millimeter from this mechanical uniformity of its prose. For example: to avoid any rising or falling in tone, the graph of this book would have to be a horizontal line that barely undulates at all; everything passed on to the reader must thus be already totally assimilated. Never may we see a progression! So whether it's the sentiments or the critical interpretations, all the prose must be unified to the referent style, and this style must stay in place long after the events in the story but even longer after they are interpreted within the story. The use of the conservative and humorous idiom must be constant, never a tossed-off expression, along with the previously mentioned rules against any transgressions in grammar or syntax. Not one allowed! Not the slightest suspicion of anything of the sort can be allowed to hover over these pages.

A mainstream American magazine or newspaper would

---

1. Mary McCarthy (1912–1989), the noted literary and social critic and novelist.

ask of its contributors exactly all of these things, a stylistic regimentation of exactly this type. "La McCarthy" shows us therefore a "style" journalistic to the hilt, but so sure of itself, full of such transparent desire to be so journalistic, that it comes off almost as "gusto" by the process diametrically opposite to the very definition of "gusto" writing; in other words, instead of the oozing chaos of magma, here we have the aseptic order of the production line.

And this is the enigma against which, as against a wall white and shining, the reader like an insect in a frenzy continually bashes his head.

By the middle of the book, at any rate, the idea you get is that we're dealing with a prose-poem, but this prose, in contrast to the usual, isn't poetic: it's true prose, this prose, but exactly, of the daily newspaper.

As for the contents of this prose-poem, one thinks (again toward the middle of the book), that it could be a pragmatic "portrait" of American pragmatism, a profound identification, through sympathy or understanding, between portraitist and subject portrayed. So the events and actions which are the height of self-sufficient pragmatism are joined to a writing style itself a part of pragmatic self-sufficiency. It's true it's not possible to avoid a "detachment," of course in this case theorized and well-applied, between the writer and the "pragma" she describes; but even this detachment is a pragmatic detachment. This is how even something that contradicts pragmatism can still be practical (in reality AND in this book)—this being the categorical imperative (Kant).

And it's exactly toward the middle of the book where we see take shape, as if it were a discovery by the reader, this humble hypothesis: in this "prose-poem" of La McCarthy, the content is a drama that unrolls between a hero on a grand scale and pragmatism, and all this in the conscience of a boy, the son of an American mother and a Jewish-Italian father (they're divorced).

And what else but, after a while, we see that Kant, as this invisible antagonist, in his rare and decisive appearances, becomes pragmatic, even him! And how? By way of idealism, which isn't the opposite of pragmatism, just its other face. And this—make no mistake—is what allows certain Americans to be pacifists, to join up with SNCC, to fight . . . against the establishment of a power pretty close to fascism, without, for all this, ceasing to be Americans.

Peter, the boy protagonist, doesn't live a drama therefore, but a perpetual and incurable crisis of conscience. The same as was lived by the middle class of his parents' day, racist and imperialist, in re-establishing balance broken by cynicism and the brutality of commerce first, and industrialization after, by way of the invention of honesty (protestantism, puritanism, etc.).

All this seems to be our own discovery reading the book, but at the end, on the last page, I say on the very LAST page, as in cheap novels (even so, this is one stupendous page) we come to realize that all this was projected and calculated by La McCarthy: and that the shadow of Kant, seated at the foot of Peter's bed . . . feverish because of a bird bite, assumes a function strictly pragmatic in announcing to Peter the "Death of Nature."

And so? A book that we, in the Italian circuit, would call naturalistic, an unending (374 pages) slice of life, suddenly reveals itself as allegorical or, at least, heavily metaphorical? But it doesn't have dimensions, body, character, tone, proportions, "suspense"—nothing, zero!

At the end, looking over our shoulder at the events of the book, it's true that we can get a sense of metaphor: but while this sense, page by page, even though only described indirectly by the infinite variety of the events, seems profoundly significant, even if standing aside a bit from the usual sense of the word (as shared by the entire international *intelligentsia*), at the end this aspect (the death of nature caused by total industrialization) perhaps interests us less precisely for being already "things common to all," like the sea (polluted). But here's what's more interesting: the idea that all this ponderous prose we had to read to reach this conclusion is interesting just because of all its obsession with daily factual details (too many; since she's being journalistic, even if she's writing exactly according to the canons of journalistic prose, this stuff renders the story strangely ambiguous and maybe a little weird).

The interest of this long story makes itself felt in two thrusts. The first is regarding the mother (La fata Rosamund), the second the son (Peter). But since this book succeeds even in its mysterious way to construct a whole world, with its internal cohesion of facts and above all its "tempo," we have its first part (the mythical period of Rocky Point lived in intimacy between mother and son) finish by appearing to be objectively in the distance, magically shrouded in mystery. As such, defeated in these years, walled off in memories that fade and get romanticized more and more with respect to reality (which one finds always brutally in the present), Rosamund effectively ends up less of an interesting person for us. And from her we're left with, just like a benevolent nightmare, her obsession with searching shops for old objects and food items you can't find anymore (the death of nature).

So how can I tell you at this point in regard to this book

that's not exactly *The Sentimental Education*, or *Ulysses*, nor even *The Wanderer*, that Peter is an extraordinary character? Is it possible to construct a grand portrait using common material with not much in the way of artistic pedigree? Can you reconcile a grand literary figure with literature so (consciously, to be sure) journalistic?

The fact is that Peter is drawn out slowly, slowly like a person charged with an absolutely rare potential for reality. Perhaps this is the point of contact between reality as pragmatically lived and reality as pragmatically written. Peter is exactly as he would be if we had actually known him, physically seen and observed him. The pragmatism of someone totally steeped in it allows La McCarthy to write a loose chronicle, full of prosaic "high culture," inflated until one's had enough. But the result is to have pragmatism transmitted by the people and things in the book in such a way that they reappear in the imagination of the reader almost unrelated to the pages where the reader saw them. La McCarthy has toured the U.S.A. and the American's Europe and done it a little like Salimene toured the Po Valley.

This is how Peter is physically, how he does things, how he dresses and speaks, how he comforts himself, is alive and more a part of an existential experience than a literary one.

In addition, he's a personality rather exceptional and emblematic: he's half-Jewish, half-Italian and thus "ethnic," educated in a family that is one of the opposition for its beliefs (rigidly puritan), and at the same time, he's extremely ordinary in the sense that he's not distinct enough to stand out in a crowd or be put in a category; so, entering into him, into his divided interior, which doesn't monologue but rather dialogues dramatically with himself, we enter into the mechanism of an enigma.

People like Peter are in fact the most unknown, precisely

for being neither part of the "petty-bourgoisie" nor of the "elite" (or at least their families are *no longer* "elite"), but rather part of that nebulous army of "beautiful spirits" (with all due respect to their sensitivity and rigorous ingenuousness) who determine, in spite of their continual defeats, public opinion, and make possible the existence of a high "culture," of an art scene, of a literature. They are the "literate" and it is to them that an intellectual speaks and recognizes as brothers for a certain series of characteristics they share, while the very thing that makes them distinct and often his moral superiors escapes him, as it's a very difficult thing to mix interest in the truly exceptional with a "common" life lived in humble anonymity.

The life of the adolescent Peter is told to us via a bunch of episodes. Taken one by one, none of these are exceptional, even though related "to perfection" by the author. But the motive for this prioritizing of certain episodes above others seems to be unconsciously consistent and regular: to describe Peter's solitude. His wholesome education as a boy, that of the heroic boy scout, i.e., you confront everything you need to confront, *just like anybody else*, is an education that establishes him, mitigating his status as an "ethnic" (which he has in spite of his innocent ordinariness and which makes you want to hug him, what with that skinniness and that big Jewish nose). Turning one's attention inward, looking at the series of episodes that, strangely unending, linger on as a presence over the shoulder of the reader who has finished the book (on the day of the first bombing of North Vietnam), with the vague intention of balancing things out, what you're left with is a longstanding atrocity lived by a protagonist with a "good will" that tugs at your heart.

1973. Translated by Jonathan Richman

101 Zen Stories

Marcel Granet, *The Religion of the Chinese*

It's evident I can say very little critically plausible about a small book that gathers 101 Zen stories. I don't know anything about it because of my instinctive rejection of things that come from fashion beyond any form—even the most basic—of historicism. I was never interested in Zen. Now that I read this small book, it's as if in my hand I had a fist of sand, and starting from this fist of sand I were expected to say something about the desert. What I can say, if I want to, is very subjective and generic, and it's that at least half of these stories are sublime. As for the text, I can also intervene technically, but like an artisan who observes a product produced by the artisanship of another culture. The language (which I don't believe the translation's changed or betrayed) is very spare and precise; the syntax is elementary; the simplicity, more than that of fairy tales, is one of scientific divulgation; it has the brevity of the "haiku," about which there is a perfect description inside the text: "In the first verse there's the premise; in the second there's the continuation of that premise; the third verse distances itself from the topic and starts a new one; and the fourth connects the other three. "A popular Japanese song goes:

The daughters of a silk merchant live in Kyoto
The oldest is twenty years old, the youngest eighteen.
A soldier can also kill with his sword.
But these girls kill men with their eyes.

Often—in these short stories—the premise and the "continuation of the premise" are summaries of actual novels: stories of movies for Mizoguchi or Ichikawa. For example, "Zenkai, the son of a samurai, went to Edo and entered that city along with a senior official. He fell in love with the wife of an official and was caught. To defend himself he killed the official. Then he runs away with the official's wife. After that the two became thieves. But the woman was so greedy that Zenkai started to nourish a real aversion to her. . . ."

The final twist of all these short stories, as is known, is a light mockery turning the situation, the confirmation, upside down, or vice versa: fixing the elements of absolute ambiguity (something completely contrary, and yet similar, to the notion of Necessity in Greek culture). Behind this philosophic "joy," derived from the cult of nothingness, remains the idea of life as a duty to fulfill, and thus the cult of praxis: one has to meditate but also one has to do. This extreme contradiction brings to extreme tension the Ambiguity. Meaning that in the text a phenomenon materializes that seems to me the most typical: the continuous recourse to a system of signs that's different from the linguistic one, meaning the mimetic system, changing the verbal communicative relationship to a pragmatic relationship of scenic action. To a university professor who asked what was Zen, the master Nan-in answered by pouring tea in a cup till the tea started to overflow (meaning: the head of the professor was already full of ideas, it needed to be emptied out before engaging in a new science). Another master, Hotei, used to go around with a sack. To one who asked about the meaning of Zen, Hotei answered by putting the sack down. To the next question, what is the implementation of Zen? Hotei answered by putting his sack back on his shoulder and resuming walking. Another master made a dissolute nephew lace up the master's sandal and thus let him understand that there's always a moment in life in which a human being is in need of the other. "Parables lived out" in these ways are the most frequent schemata of these short stories. The mimetic system doesn't naturally substitute for the verbal one, but even it is always meant, in some way, theatrically. The cue triumphs: the briefer it is, the more efficient it will be. A saint, finding his mother dead, starts a brief dialogue with her, reciting her part as well, a total of three lines.

This theatrical sense—even if extremely discreet, restrained, laconic—of the human relationships, contains both acceptance and mockery of such relationships: the pragma—seen above the lines, carried out in principle—and the nothingness—felt as the other face of acting, with its practical imperatives—render one another ineffable, since they coexist, negating themselves. So language is used with skepticism and yet with the extreme lightness of a small brush that paints on silk.

This linguistic impossibility of going beyond certain limits or layers of reality, especially psychological, and the subsequent necessity of preaching about the void with silence, results also from the study of the ancient Chinese religion: the pagan religion that is anterior to the historical religious reforms, namely of Buddha and Confucius. This pagan religion, even if it's similar to all peasant religions, was, however, strangely without myths, legends, theogonies. Marcel Granet (from whom I derive my notions), in a book that talks about the religion of the Chinese, explains that with the impossibility of the Chinese language to clearly distinguish adjective from noun, and noun from verb, we have a language that's purely practical, incapable of designing myth with limpidity, a language for which liturgical clarity of action is necessary and the stereotypical use of adjectives is necessary, among other things. We shouldn't be surprised if the Chinese tradition (where Zen was born, with the name Ch'an) asserts that Buddha preached for 40 years without saying a single word.

In spite of that, the Chinese religion and the Japanese religion are basically rational and practical. If Zen during these years has been fashionable in the Western world, it's not because of Zen's exotic appeal or alternativeness. Rather, for Westerners it's been the confirmation of the goodness of *their* rational and practical spirit.

Recently I found myself in the center of the Orient, so much in the center of it that I can say that I was in the center of the center or, if you will, at the bottom of the bottom. A plane that was supposed to bring me directly from New Delhi to Nepal landed in Benares, and from there, I don't know for what reason, it never took off again; a new plane was promised for the day after but, because of a series of recent experiences that weren't very reassuring, I wasn't trusting that promise; so I decided to go to Katmandu by car. After two hours and a hundred kilometers in the car on a road that leads to Calcutta, we left that particular road and started to head north, and when it was already deep night we reached Patna, the capital of Bihar. The morning after we left for Nepal through the Bihar plain, we weren't too far from the city where Buddha was born. This time around, but only when it was deep night, first through mountains covered by a marvelous virgin forest, then on the naked slopes of the Himalayas, we reached the Katmandu valley.

Even though very Westernized, meaning that its architecture remained only in relics or in the hybrid due to misery, Bihar is the most exotic region I've ever seen: perhaps precisely because it's without any folklore (there aren't temples or fortresses; the dung or mud huts basically have no shape; the houses of the city are amassed one next to the other, with their ancient design, but they are completely deformed by metal sheets and plastic objects, etc.). The weather was cloudy, the sky was mirroring itself in wild puddles. An immense crowd was going around in the muddy morning silence. Many were washing themselves on the banks of the Ganges, yellowish, dirty, sad. They were going up and down along the bank covered with modern objects, pieces of engines, pipes, oil stains, amid ancient small huts or bunches of vegetable gardens. They were all carrying in their hands the small brass vases in which they were saving the Ganges water for the day. Where were they going? In all the days of their lives there wasn't even a single moment of peace, of commodity, of intimacy waiting for them. They could lie down on a dirty doormat on the muddy floor of their houses: here they could find the maximum moment of peace that was allowed them. They couldn't have any other shelter from a life lived among the crowd than that of covering their faces with an eternally dirty rag. But their looks, their words, their gestures were familiar to me; they were even very prosaically human. They smiled with the usual smiles that you can see in the outskirts of big cities: with sweetness, with cunning, with anxiety. Around them, threats of famine and cholera were looming, exactly at the point at which they are about to become real. And deep inside them, to guide their gestures and their feelings, there was a religion degenerated into superstition disgusting for a contemporary man (at the corner of a small house next to the ferry, in the mud, there was a dry chunk of wood with its rotten roots and, in the middle of it, a small Buddha statue with some offerings, some soaked flowers, some food, and other indefinable materials—even as they were somehow fascinating). Filthiness, boundless immensity, desperation, resignation were making Bihar a sort of "elsewhere" through which one can only pass as a stranger, even if recognizing the brotherhood of those people whose ancient way of being was rendering them rather familiar.

To arrive from there to Nepal was like coming back. Coming back home, where everything is less unraveled but more cruel, stupendous Katmandu, city of red bricks, like Ferrara, with big wooden balconies like Austria; the streets covered with blond hay, the cornices of the houses full of vases, and vegetables that are there to dry; the rustic temples, of poor materials but sublimely elegant (bricks covered by grass and wood); the deep fountains made like a flight of stairs, where women go to wash; the thousand tabernacles with their bronze bells that ring like ours. . . . Nepal is the "cradle" of the Chinese civilization, like the Nile is for the Western one. A feudal and peasant civilization. Emerging from the depth of India, to trace the Oriental margins is like tracing the Western margins. The Orient is the bottom of the funnel in which religions are tragically born as an absolute state, expanding toward the margins, the West or the Far East; these religions lose their ascetic absoluteness: they reach a compromise with practical activity, with reason. For example, the idea or the feeling of Nothingness (after all unspeakable) both in the philosophies of the stoic-epicurean type or empiric—in the West—and in Zen—the Far East—certainly also means the presence of a cosmic Nothingness, but it's most of all a social nothingness. Reason doesn't let itself be destroyed by social nothingness. Social nothingness wants to destroy reason because social nothingness invents and accepts objectivities. But the contrary actually occurs: reason takes possession of it, reinforcing in the confrontation its certitude of being: nothing is more resistant and solid than what is ambiguous. Ambiguously mocking reality invented and manipulated by reason, both Western and Chinese or Japanese reason make themselves coincide not only with the whole but also with nothingness.

1973. Translated by Flavio Rizzo

CAMPANA AND POUND

Why did right-wing literature seize on a poet like Dino Campana? I mean to allude, for example—in reference to a recent popular re-edition of all of Campana's work—to Enrico Falqui, diligent and sharp curator of the works, to Mario Luzi, who wrote the preface to the volume and to one of its sections (the correspondence between Campana and Aleramo), to Silvio Ramat and Domenico De Robertis, who wrote the texts' glosses. Almost without exception, the body of criticism devoted to Campana—from the 25th of December 1914 (Bino Binazzi) to the 20th of March 1973 (Pietro Bianchi)—has been written by men belonging to the literary (and often even political) right. Only a small number of "left" writers and critics are included, but up to this moment, ingenuously, they've always ended up playing into the hands of those people who, through Campana, tried to create a "progressive" alibi for themselves while not even cynically organizing an *opening to the Left*. Is there something in Campana that justifies all this?

Today, when we reread all Campana's work, the first reality that enters our mind is the simple reality that this crazy person, this wild poet, was a learned man: there's no page, line, or single word in his production without the unmistakable "sound" of culture. He was roughly learned, of course, but basically educated. He studied chemistry at Bologna's University and he stubbornly kept on with studies that didn't suit him, so his literary culture wasn't exactly professional, but neither was it that kind of culture of perhaps genial self-taught persons. I mean, his relation with reality and literature and the metalinguistic relation with his own work were basically rational. His pictorial culture was particularly precise: the contributions of cubist taste and figurative futurism in his language are impeccable. Some of his brief poems—still lifes—are among the most successful, and when they are "in the manner of," they have a skillful critical taste. Even the surrealist background of his poetry in prose is recovered without confusions or *wild ambitions*: on the contrary, it's recovered with an extraordinary calm (*The Night* is perhaps Campana's best work). Finally, even the critical judgments, which are, however, very rare, of his contemporaries, and the oddly-shaped *commas* for a possible manifesto of his own literary theory (in the fashion of those years)—even in their induced madness "to shock the bourgeoisie," are particularly limpid, lively, successful.

At the same time, there was his madness (that madness that led him to long hospitalizations, and at the same time to those travels as an ancient "biante"[1] or as an amazingly prefigured hippie, even in the most literal sense of the word): in fact Campana twice narcissistically describes himself as "cappellone," and "poveta cappellone":[2] he spells the word with two "p's," but this doesn't prevent the reader from shivering. Campana's *exegetes* and biographers did well in not giving any account of his madness. Pity? Discretion? Bourgeois prissiness? Fear of wasting the eventual mystery and a certain spirituality attributed, actually, to madness? Whatever it was, the only documents on Campana's illness are his own texts, and some testimonies that only the reader's diagnostic acumen can assume as relevant: for example, his father's testimony, when it tells of his teenage son's violent outbursts of hatred against his mother (that poor

---

1. "Biante": ancient italian spelling for "viandante," wanderer.
2. "Poveta cappellone": spelling for "poeta capellone," hippie poet.

Fanny Campana, elementary schoolteacher, of whom we read some very nice, tough, almost illiterate, letters in the Campana-Aleramo correspondence), and of course all the testimonies regarding his escapes. Those escapes, indeed, very likely are escapes from the mother. That mother who will be mythically recovered in those monumental figures of bawds rather more than of prostitutes.

Not knowing what kind of mental disease Campana suffered from, we can't study its aphasic contributions in the texts—the obsessive linguistic preferences and the eventual exclusions. But, on one hand, we've seen that his linguistic choices *occur as marks* of the most self-confident literary taste. His "fragmentariness" could be a symptom of a pathological aphasic form: but it's not, because it coincides with one of the most fixed and unquestionable canons of the time. On the other hand, even his pre-fascist rhetoric—the way he felt "Germanic"—or "German," as he says—and the subsequent racist phobia toward Italian meridionality[3]—were parts of that particular cultural "reactionarism" of the early 20th century that shouldn't be considered literally. Campana's attitude was in fact reactionary, but antinational: and so?

In spite of Campana's great human sympathy, and of the complexity of his cultural personality, when we finish reading his work, we feel disappointed: we feel like we've arrived at owning a basically useless "palimpsest" (Pound): it gratifies us, not only with pity (and this is good), but even with something that remains hopelessly objective. Campana's knowledge can't be assimilated. Moreover, the reading turns into the ghost of

---

3. The reference is to exclusion—at times at a racial level—of the south of Italy by the north.

Campana, the same who looks lost at his reader, not knowing how to make himself be forgiven for the poverty of that knowledge he drew from his existence, a knowledge that remained private and useless even for himself. So we remain with this speechless gaze upon us, with the author staring at us, more to ask us for help—from the bottom of the iterative senseless mediocrity of the whole of his work—than to reproach us for attributing to him an impotence that, he well knows, belongs to him. It's this basic harmlessness in facing the real that's used by right-wing culture, which immediately seized upon Campana. The right's madness has always been formal and rhetorical: finally they were able to find a "real" crazy person to fit their interests. Even with all the catholic precaution of the case, and with the usual hypocritical pity—in the face of Campana's incapacity to restore that reality which he narcissistically attacked without even believing the results of this aggression—traditional literate Italian readers (hermetic readers in reality) saw in him the living expression—but not a literally, socially, or politically dangerous one; of their own spiritualistic and delirious *Nietzschean* aspiration to the interior superman—that's how they deformed a poetry that, on the contrary, is basically realistic, even if inspired by a stifling aestheticism.

It's outrageous that madness, making the crazy person harmless, leaves him to the embrace and the protection of the most interested and cunning people. It's the same case with Pound. It's true that Pound's reactionary statements go far beyond a dedication to "William II, Emperor of Germany," but certainly they're no less unreliable. A few months ago Scheiwiller published Pound's economic essays "against usury," whose arguments return and obsessively repeat themselves in all the *Cantos*, leaving in fact no doubt about the author's state of confusion.

Pound's reactionary ideology is due to his rustic background, as Campana's is. Behind Campana, there's Marradi,[4] the poor Romagna of the early 20th century, land and laborers, socialism and anarchy: but doubtless what still mattered, above everything, was the universe of the "eternal return" (see in this regard the *Whiteshirt* volumes by Mircea Eliade, who is an illustrious scholar of religions), from which people could escape only by "breaking the egg" (this was the highest moment in the orphic mystery). Behind Pound there was instead the immensity of the rustic United States, of which we know nothing except grandiose and confused events and situations. What's certain is that immigrants in America were Latin or Irish *sub-proletarian* farmers, and so they brought their own universes, so different yet so similar at the same time, but all equally archaic universes. On the contrary, we have to suppose that farming in the United States over a century ago, when Pound's father was more or less in his 20s, was very different from working the fields in Calabria or in Ireland. We learned what aspects of this farmers' world entered in Pound—by means of his father and of his grandfather's mythical image—through the idealization he made of Chinese culture: an idealization that in fact develops from that archaic rustic world of modern American farmers. Pound (as well as Campana, despite his book's title)[5] is in no way an orphic poet. He madly and strongly wanted to remain always inside the rustic world: he even wanted to go deeper and deeper into it and more and more towards its center.

His ideology consists of nothing but the veneration of the rustic world's values (which were practically revealed to him by means of the pragmatic and virtuous Chinese culture). In this

4. Marradi is the small town near Florence where Campana was born.
5. *Orphic Poems.*

sense I think we could subscribe, even politically, to all Pound's conservative verses aiming to exalt (with furious nostalgia) the rustic world's rules and the cultural unity between the Lord and the servants: "The fatherly word is compassion / filial, devotion; / the brotherly one, mutuality; / tosatel's (young boy's) word is respect." And also: "The king loves to plow, from the *alpha* / the Empress cares for the trees with veneration, / neither do they avoid the warm duties . . ." And also: "There is worship in plowing."

Critics tried to give a united appearance to the *Cantos'* accumulation, attributing to them a "plot," a little like with Joyce's *Ulysses*, that was left at a fragmentary stage, eternally interrupted by excursus, parenthesis, and disproportionate deviations that in the end made this eventual unity seem invisible. But doubtless there's a plot in the *Cantos*, even if it's not to be sought in the sequence of the written material, but rather in its depth: as Pound himself says ("there is a nexus indeed / even if my notes make no sense"): the *Cantos'* "nexus" consists in a march backward into the heart of the rustic world (whose symbol is ancient China), where governments get more and more tyrannical and enlightened, the world more and more practical and idealist, and "Filiation, fraternity: are the roots, / Talents are the boughs / Terminology the first instrument / litre and bushel. / Thereafter: nine arts! / Classics, / virtuous history / totally candid."

Also at the end of reading the *Cantos*, we feel emptied and also disappointed. Their knowledge is too particular and tragically private to actually be able to enlarge our cultural patrimony. Behind us there's a man (not even looking at us) whose experience has been impoverished by a sort of—organic, mental—incapacity to flow with even desperate fullness. Pound knows that well and, in Canto CXVI, as in a sort of testament, he says: "Charity sometime I had, I can't make it flow. . . ."

But even if it doesn't communicate to us a knowledge of some use, because of its "deviancy," at least Pound's work communicates to us delirium's pure experience. No reading in the world is so inebriating as Pound's reading. Reading Canto LXXVI has the effect that, I suppose, the most powerful and wonderful drug must have. Pound could never openly become a right-wing prerogative: his very high culture, even if, in the American way, a bit elementary (when he landed in Europe during the first years of the century, he considered himself a "barbarian"), prevented him from an impudent use: the big (disgusting) fascist snake could not swallow this sacrificial Easter lamb. But impalpable fascist preoccupations have always surrounded him, as now they surround his memory. Before all this and everyone else there was his daughter, Mary de Rachewiltz. One will never be able to deprecate this situation enough. Mary de Rachewiltz—who was educated in Alto Adige by a nurse, according to the precepts of a country moralism that could only be deleterious for a bourgeois woman frustrated by her illegitimacy; who was educated in the last years of fascist Italy; and who served as a Red Cross worker in a Nazi Hospital until the last days of the war—not only manages and arrogantly monopolizes—as mediocre translator—her father's poetic capital, but moreover she writes a book of testimonies about him: I don't remember ever reading such a dumb and factious book (in spite of a lot of evasiveness). Of course what could be interesting in such a book was exactly Pound's relation with fascism, but Mary de Rachewiltz not only didn't understand anything of her father and of fascism, but she doesn't even question the subject.

1973. Translated by Giada Diano

IGNAZIO BUTTITTA, "I ACT THE POET"

For a long time now, I've repeated how I have been feeling this great nostalgia for poverty, mine and other people's, and that we're mistaken to consider poverty an evil. These are reactionary statements that nevertheless I knew I was making from an extreme left-wing position, even if it was a position still not defined and certainly not easy to define. Here in the sadness of seeing myself surrounded by a population I don't recognize anymore, by a young generation left unhappy, neurotic, aphasic, obtuse, and presumptuous by the extra 1,000 lire that a good economy's suddenly dropped into their pocket, comes the arrival of austerity programs, obligatory poverty. Now, I consider government austerity programs to be downright unconstitutional, I'm infuriated me to think of how this stuff is done in conjunction with the Holy Year. But as a warning sign of the return of real poverty, it can only make me happy. Mind you, I say *poverty*, not misery; I'm ready for whatever personal sacrifice this means, naturally. But it'll be worth it to see that old-time smile on peoples' faces, that old respect for other people that was really self-respect. The pride in being what the old-time "poor" culture taught them to be. Then one could maybe start over again. I'm raving here, I realize. For sure, the current economic restrictions, which have an air of permanency about them—setting up a style of living to become the future for us all—can only mean one thing: that too easy was the prophecy desperately hoping that the study of humanity would be that of industrialization total and for the good of all. That is, "another story," in which neither the current way of living nor the reasoning of Marxism would make sense anymore, will be what happens. Maybe the climax of this aberrant stage, even though we don't dare hope it, has already happened, and we're starting back down the parabolic curve. Men, then, will maybe have to re-experience their past after having artificially risen above it in a kind of fever, a frenetic unconsciousness.

Certainly, as I read in Piovene,[1] retrieving this past will go badly at first, a bad mixture of the new comfort and the old misery. But even this world of chaos and confusion, this "dressing down," is welcome. Anything is better than this way of life our society has been so dizzily building.

Suddenly in this situation, after almost 30 years, I've started writing in the Friulian dialect again. Maybe I'll not continue this. The few verses I've done are maybe a "unicum." Anyway they're a symptom and as such a sign of an irreversible phenomenon. I didn't have a car when I was writing in dialect (first Friulian, then Roman). Not a penny in my pocket and I traveled by bike. And this at 30 years of age and more. It wasn't just youthful poverty. In all the poor societies around me, dialect seemed destined not to be lost, except in a future so far away as to seem abstract. The Italianization of Italy seemed to depend on ample support from the grassroots, with dialect and vernacular a big part of this (and not on the substitution of literary language with corporate language, as has happened recently). Among the other tragedies we've borne (and which I've felt personally, sensually) in these last years, we add the tragedy of the loss of dialect as one of the saddest moments in our loss of reality (which in Italy has always been distinctive, eccentric, earthy, never centralized, never "establishment").

This purging of dialect, and of the particular culture of each

---

1. Guido Piovene, a leading writer and journalist of the time.

dialect, represented a loss due to the new power of the consumer society in our culture, the most centralizing kind of power, and thus the most substantially fascist, as history reminds us. This is explicitly the theme of a poem by a dialect poet titled "Language and Dialect" ("Lingua e Dialettu") (the poet is Igancio Buttitta, the dialect is Sicilian).

The people are always fundamentally free and rich: They can be chained, stripped, gagged, but they're basically free; you can take their job, passport, even the table they eat on, but they're more or less free. Why? Because they have their own culture, and to have this vehicle to express yourself is to be free and rich, even if what you are expressing (in relation to the ruling class) is misery and a lack of freedom.

Culture and economic conditions are perfectly coincident. A poor culture (agricultural, feudal, provincial) "knows" really only its own economic conditions, and from that vantage point, it articulates poorly, but according to the infinite complexity of existence. Only when something foreign infiltrates (something that now happens almost all the time with the constant contact with totally different economic conditions), *then* that culture will be in crisis. In agricultural societies, this crisis causes "class awareness" (an awareness always haunted by the specter of regression). The crisis is therefore a crisis of those judging their own way of life, less certain of their own values, which then grows into outright rejection (this, exactly, happened in Sicily in recent years, caused by mass emigration of youth to Germany and Northern Italy). A symbol of this "deviation" (so brutal and not at all revolutionary) of their cultural tradition, is the annihilation and humiliation of dialect, which, even though it remains intact statistically—spoken by the same number of people—is no longer a way of being nor a cultural value. The guitar of dialect loses a string every day. Dialect has still got lots of money it can no longer spend and has little jewels it can no longer bequeath. He who speaks it is like a bird who sings but in a cage. Or like a tit that everybody has sucked on and now they spit on (rejection!). What cannot be robbed (yet) is the body, with its vocal cords, voice, articulation, manner, which stay on as before. But that's mere survival. Even though we're still in possession of this mysterious organ "with its lights in its eyes" which is the body, "we're poor and orphaned just the same."

This poem, so perfectly tragic, has an equivalent in another poem titled "The Rancors." Also here the conclusion (expressively perfect) doesn't leave any hope at all. The poet, dialectical and popular (in the Gramscian sense), gathers the sentiments of the poor, their "rancor," their rage, their explosion of hatred: he acts, in sum, as their interpreter, their translator; but he, the poet, is a bourgeois. A bourgeois who keeps his privileged status, who wants peace in his house so as to forget the wars in the other houses, who is a dog of the same breed as the oppressors. He doesn't want for anything, is lacking nothing but a crown to recite the rosary at night, and there is no one who'll bring an iron wire to hang him from a pole.

Before, however, this "no way out" conclusion, perfectly and sadistically clear, the entire body of the poem is founded on reticence, like a rhetorical figure whose meaning is what it denies. And what does Buttitta deny, repeatedly, even anaphorically? He denies that he, the poet, feels the rancor, the hate, anger, and sense of injustice in the confrontations with the class in power. He suggests that all these sentiments are the people's, that the poet does nothing but interpret. But for all that, Buttitta only proves the opposite. And why?

Because dominating his book is a rhetorical figure of the

masses drawn from a great inaugural model, and to this model brought back. This model is ambiguous, but only superficially. It's the model expressed by the Russian revolutionary years, with two main styles: formalism and socialist realism.

The quick strokes Buttitta uses to sketch "the people" are the same as one of those super-formal stylized posters. The meter, which mimics the oratory of flag-bedecked podiums, instead expresses the same analytical brushstrokes used to depict "the masses" on one of those socialist-realist posters.

This is because the poet, rather than be judged as a bourgeois, practices himself the things he preaches to the masses. Buttitta can't in fact be unaware that the masses, especially the Sicilian masses (not to be denied their capacities for revolt and rage), were never reconciled with the image the historical Communist Party had of them.

But this *served* the parties for their political tactics and, in a second instance, *served* the poets who could thus sing of such tactics. The poet who wrote "Language and Dialect" could not have been anything but aware of this. And yet, describing the masses the way he describes them, namely conventionally and almost falsely, Buttitta isn't being at all insincere. A similar depiction of the masses, renewed with a passion equal to its precision from the Communist style of the early part of the 20th century, was part of Buttitta's direct, that is to say, formal inspiration.

He'd always wanted to be part of Communist officialdom: and there's nothing that encourages stylizing more than an officialdom not yet in power and, in some cases, still almost oppositional and clandestine.

Neruda (quoted by Sciascia,[2] who did the preface to this

---

2. Leonardo Sciascia has become one of Italy's leading novelists and short-story writers.

book by Buttitta) is the quintessential example of this kind of poetry. But while Neruda is a bad poet, this humble man of Bagheria—sentimental, extroverted, innocent, and, in that archetype of "poetry of the people," the "malnato" or "lowly born," haunted by a lack of maternal affection that left him orphaned and obsessed—is the one you'd call a good poet. The stylized figure of the masses who, "in a Guttusian light"[3] throng his poems with closed fists and banners, becomes perfectly real if you see them (as they couldn't have been seen any other way by the man who wrote "Lingua e Dialittu") as not of these times.

Meaning that the world they belong to was the one where dialect was spoken, and now no one speaks it except with embarrassment; where they wanted revolution but now that's been forgotten; where once there was in any event a grace (and a violence) which now they renounce.

1974. Translated by Jonathan Richman

---

3. Adjective formed from the name of Reynaldo Guttuso, the great Sicilian activist painter.

CONSTANTINE CAVAFIS, *HIDDEN POEMS*

I had barely finished writing that simply mentioning homo-
sexuality is "taboo"—as we used to say with that awkward and
by now abused word—when Filippo M. Pontani's preface to
Cavafis' *Hidden Poems* gives me a sad confirmation.

The little page he dedicates to this great poet's eroticism
(I consider him, with Apollinaire and Antonio Machado, the
greatest poet of the early 20th century) is the masterpiece of an
Ephesian fanatical about Saint Paul. And Pontani is a superb
scholar, a learned man. At least, he's Cavafis' man; we owe our
knowledge of Cavafis to his care: "umbra world," "soul darkened
and empty, with an inexplicable hesitation on the threshold of a
contact with the senses," "an obsessive whirling of unexpressed
memories," "fleeting meetings in a bar," "a *strange beauty* in a
theatre," "glimpsed or remembered figures," and, finally, men-
tioned with almost dismaying audacity, "the Greek pleasure."
Who is the addressee of these ambiguous utterances between
the masculine and the feminine? Pontani himself? The reader?
Undoubtedly, there's something in Cavafis' text that can be as-
sumed as the "model" of these hesitations (which, in an Italian
context, are definitively flowery): but, first of all, it deals with
Cavafis' relation with an idealized or badly imagined Western
reader, mainly English (puritan, maybe even Victorian); and
secondly, it deals with the openly ambiguous vision Cavafis has
of history (always according to English late romanticism and
British patterns of decadence). All of this becomes sublimely
"softened" in Cavafis; and the reticence is Mozartian, that is,
gloomy, coquettish ("They're Gods for gaiety," says Gemisto—
quoted by Pound). But to be afraid of mentioning Cavafis' love

for young people means not to love Cavafis. All the more so be-
cause the Greek-Alexandrian and Levantine world Cavafis lived
in undoubtedly didn't have this kind of shame.

Cavafis practically had sex as often and as much as he
wanted: homosexual love was accepted in his world. In a certain
way it was indeed honored (among other things, it's still so: at
least, until consumerist Age tolerance doesn't oblige that world
to renounce it, according to the habit of the times of so-called
underdevelopment). So Cavafis didn't have to face problems of
social order—with their blame—because of his pederasty: he
wasn't *tolerated*, he was free—of course all of this to the extent
that he wasn't becoming Westernized. His Westernizing culture
implied also the puritan and hypocritical idea of blame. Euro-
centrism has its bedrock in the false "dignity" of the man who
has a false idea of himself. One gives up to human weaknesses
or he follows the rules; or one puts on a lot of airs (the powerful
people, the priests), as ingenuously as the simple people who,
on the contrary, surrender them, indeed, to ingenuous human
weaknesses. The eventual religious condemnation (truly, almost
always purely nominal) never becomes moralist. This ingenuous
and ingenuously degraded and corrupted world shows perfectly
through Cavafis' poems. It's never a feeling of guilt by Cavafis
or by the boy he likes, which interrupts or makes their relation-
ship painful: it's the simple case of life, as happens between a
man and a woman. Of course relationships with a boy tend al-
ways to be either aprioristically lighter or aprioristically more
tragic than with a woman. Love for a boy can't, on one hand, be
blessed, legitimized; on the other hand it's condemned to the
physical transformation of the boy who grows up and acquires
new sexual characteristics. So Cavafis couldn't but live the anx-
iousness of libertinage and the subsequent loneliness. With an

immense pain, with a pain equal to the joy that was, in reality, streaming through all of his life.

As happens with Sandro Penna, on the other hand, all Cavafis' poems have a constant and secret sense: the idea of existence as miraculousness, discovered as through a religious "enthousiasmòs" that has characteristics both of anxiety neurosis and of euphoric neurosis. In this volume of *Hidden Poems* (the title is by the translator, as are the titles of the different sections into which the book is divided), all of Cavafis' poetic features are present in the most seductive way. In "History's Turns," Cavafis can capture amazing moments of existential substantiality, in an excess of evidence that erases almost suddenly (with poetry's barbaric energy) historical imprecision, that is suitably created for the effect of the indeed existential apparition. The talk (homily!) that resounds at the bottom of a historical fact is invented by Cavafis with the humor of a modern writer who mimes the jargonish talk of the late era (Angus Wilson or Arbasino),[1] and then outstrips it, hanging it as a "verbal idol" over the voids.

There's an atmosphere of "sacred tablets," even in the unfinished reports Cavafis gives about his lovers, in "Life's Turns." I underlined only one: *And on those beds I sprawled and lay*, where Cavafis upholds (for a Western or English writer) that the only alternative to asceticism is for a poet (however a noble possibility) to lie on beds of a particular blame—in a brothel—rather than to fraternize (that is falsely fraternize) with the other clients in the "common room." The formal perfection of all the poems (from which this one departs only for ideological

---

1. Alberto Arbasino was a member of the literary avant-garde of the '60s and of the so-called Group 63, made up of poets and writers. Some critics speculated on affinities between him and Pasolini.

reasons) seems to be due to Pontani's translation, which egre-
giously regularized and made them similar, depriving them of
their chaotic linguistic universe: a purist neo-Greek one, badly
realized, it seems (some poems are characterized, as the trans-
lator says, by "unbearable verbal rhymes"). On the contrary I
think the "situation" created for the historical poems, and cut
out for the love poems, is stronger than the page, as happens
for great novelists who *write badly*. A literary Greek language
(absurd today) couldn't but be an unsolvable problem for an
alexandrine poet of the beginning of the century. But Cavafis
doesn't "speak the word" (Lacan): he still speaks the thing.

Through a totally absurd association (Flaubert's Saint
Anthony—as failed poet—a man repressed by awful sexual
phobias in a "Levantine" society, which at that time was at the
center, not on the fringes, and was moralistic and repressive,
that is, not ingenuously understanding and corrupted—speak-
ing the minority language, Coptic, as a humiliation compared
with the culture's language, Greek, and moreover biographer
Anastasio's birth in Alexandria), I want to remember after
Cavafis, *Anthony's Life*, which was written 1500 years before.
We're in "history's turns," but Anastasio doesn't know it, and he
speaks of his Saint in a frontal way, as hagiography requires: to
him, Saint Anthony is not only not in "history's turns"; on the
contrary, he's at the center of the universe, as in an apse. While,
of course, this biography's charm depends strongly on its being
the chitchat of a bigot (in a Low Era in which the Church was
the Living Room) lost in a totally meaningless corner of history
that was swarming with paranoid hierophanies.

Another totally absurd association (history considered ac-
cording to an "aesthetic inspiration," with the stress on those
elements neglected by historians, but not perhaps by those of

religion, who on the contrary "isolate" those elements, depriving them of their objective functions) led me to read *Roman Ladies* by Pierre Klossowski. I was disappointed, almost disgusted. A book founded upon Bachofen's theories on matriarchy is justified only if it becomes exquisite and arbitrary, or elegantly outrageous. This doesn't happen at all in this pedantic little manual. Unless I'm so little ironical not to realize it's all a joke.

1974. Translated by Giada Diano

DACIA MARAINI, *MY WOMEN*

There's an initial moment in the act of reading when the eye owns everything. It's in fact known that the eye is the first instrument of possession; the eye is the creator, through introjection, of the I as propriety. Well, even the act of reading is first of all an introjection, and the eye prevails in it undisputedly. The eye ranges over the "written" page—which is always a "description" and, therefore, a statement of possession—with the barbarian conqueror's freshness.

Ranging freely over the verses of Dacia Maraini's[1] written pages, my eye immediately understood what they were about: it saw the shape of the tirade, the character of the "enjambments," the low linguistic level of *poeticalness*—about to step into prose—a use of adjectives whose expressivity, being ornamental, is merely pre-textual. After I embraced, with a glance flying as a bird, the land and its morphology to be conquered, I wondered: why did Dacia write in such an untidy way, showing such self-confidence?

The same question had entered my mind a few weeks earlier when I read Danilo Dolci's[2] book. And, indeed, there's something that links these two works by very different persons. What? Schematically it's this: the decision to leave their own books to the disposition and function of something else (political, that is, not literary, and so much more important);

---

1. Dacia Maraini, b. 1936, is today regarded as one of the leading poets of Italy. She was the companion of the great novelist Alberto Moravia (1907–1990), who was a friend of Pasolini, and they all traveled together to India.

2. A Sicilian poet and activist of the New Left in the '60s, Dolci (1924–1997) was perhaps better known in the United States as a writer than Pasolini was.

the consequent impatience for the particular effort resulting from a literary work that's so openly "overcome" by its function; the overwhelming prominent presence of the "credo," the "faith," and the consequent "loyalism," over stylistic concerns, and the introduction of mannerism as a targeted substitution for the solution of these problems. The two books share something else, at least regarding signs: the disappointment of readers' expectations, as the writers make references not to a strictly personal ideology, but to a network of ideological notions and *paraenesis*, which are already well known, codified, and belong to thought-movements to which the authors sacrifice their own personalization of the world, their own subjectivity, aesthetically nullifying themselves. In Danilo Dolci, we find the New Left, the pacifism, the radical but nonviolent contestation, etc. . . . In the whole book there's not even an idea belonging to Danilo Dolci, something that testifies, even indirectly, to the originality of his thought. His originality is committed to the action, to the intervention, *to the way one should be.* But this is exactly what the reader needed a "direct" explanation of; and his expectation can't but be disappointed by the *triumphalist* use—even if by means of a grey and depressed language—of such an abundance of current ideology.

Dacia's ideological references and her loyalty—beyond the New Left, the pacifism, the radical nonviolent contestation—definitively comprise as well that form of "renewed" Marxism that constitutes the dynamics of little groups and of what we can call the *New Demand.* In this particular case, it deals with feminism. In *His Hurry,* Dacia considered it inopportune to make true literature and to take care of the written page more than a little: she had more "serious" things to think about. She had a faith behind her. And what's the page next to faith? What happened to Dacia has been happening for centuries to catholic writers: the impatience for art, its use, its heteronomous interpretation (some pleasure together with the duty). The same thing happened to the communists in their power, at the outset, with the tremendous simplification of formalism, and later with its condemnation. Now only feminism was missing. Having women's problems and demands on his shoulders, a poet's allowed to ignore his specific morality, sacrificing it to something that, being socially more important and urgent, can't but blackmail the critic (in this case exposing him to the blame of more than half of the population of the country he lives in). Holding that a page is untidy, stretched out, only a bit adjusted in a mannerist way, becomes a guilt: the guilt of not being sensitive to the urgency of the considered subjects.

Truly, Dacia gave the reader's expectation an even greater disappointment with her book: that is, not to have brought any sincere, intelligent, and convincing contribution to the feminist cause. Above all, she accomplished a dishonest action that can't but debilitate any possible argument: it's a principle petition: the negative figure of the Italian "male" and of the "male" in general. A "male" as he appears in these verses of Dacia's doesn't exist in reality: he's totally abstract. He belongs to the comics-rhetoric of fictitiously progressive journalism. Moreover, in Dacia's verses, he's introduced as playing the role of the "wicked," fanatically lacking not only any complexity, but even any "nuance": still a comic-strip wicked. It's certain that if this kind of "wicked" actually existed, he would be very sought after: a wicked like this who arrives, taken in a raptus of almost ascetic eroticism, totally "obsessed" with the penis and the vagina, with coitus's blind violence, with sadism as slaving pretension, as a reduction of the person to the body, for popular tradition or adolescent ingenuity, etc., etc., etc., could be a sublime erotic "ideal" for certain women (and men). I know certain women and certain men who would be willing to sacrifice a fortune for a male "partner" like this. But he doesn't exist. Or he exists in a totally ridiculous way (the cock, the Latin lover), so ridiculous as to appear, in the end, moving.

Once he's liberated by this myth that makes him a guilty man, his male chauvinist ideology remains, and Dacia rightly condemns it: the problem is that the male chauvinist ideology of this man is nothing but the integration of the feminist ideology of the woman, which, on the contrary, Dacia defends. When Dacia describes traditional marriage—the virgin bride, the bridegroom who claims this virginity, the bride who doesn't know anything of coitus's mechanics and the male who knows it instead, etc., etc., etc.—she isn't describing a "victim" and a "guilt": in reality she describes two "victims" of the same social morality (generally a popular and traditional morality, shared to this day by the petty-bourgeoisie). The male claiming the bride's virginity is no less "swindled" than the bride who keeps her virginity; the male who knows (in such a context) coitus's mechanics is in reality identical to the unaware bride, as he probably will have learned these mechanics with some prostitute found in the street and held for a few minutes, etc., etc., etc.

The great solution Dacia gives women is the suggestion of covering instead of being covered, or, generally, treating coitus democratically. But I can't imagine a more disastrous or frustrating block or inhibition than introducing the duty of democracy into coitus: if, one day, it could be applied (formally) to coitus, democracy will be welcome; but "the duty of democracy" is obviously the ruin of everything, the worst of repressions.

This way of making love—perhaps precisely on the first night of the marriage—is the only contribution Dacia brings concerning the immediately revolutionary behavior of women. And it's also the only one I can—evidently not at a high level—discuss. All that remains otherwise is feminist commonplace under the dominating sign of persecution complex.

Dacia, with *Whitmanesque* countenance—corrected by a *vaguely ornamental tendency close to Lorca's*—imperializes the entire Italian female population in *My Women*. The result is a monumental sectarian attitude whose political uselessness can escape Dacia—with her mind made up—but whose total lack of cultural consistency can't.

I'd like to point out at least one real situation that Dacia could have discussed, instead of giving herself up to commonplaces, or of taking as "exempla" (which are, among the other things, the most beautiful, or better, a definitely beautiful part of the book) some women who "lived" in the classical repressive world, all well-known cases, as well-known as those of poor males, emigrants, or thieves, etc. Nowadays there are "new" young women who live "new" kinds of life and have "new" relations with peer men (especially in those places to which Dacia seems often to refer, Rome, the South).

Let's consider a block of a popular Roman neighborhood. Until a few years ago, men lived one kind of life, women another one. After twilight there wasn't any girl in the street. One *never* saw a girl in a male group. A young couple of the Roman populace kissing or making love in the gardens of the neighborhood was something inconceivable.

All boys' education occurred among males: for a young man, "the model" to realize was a popular "model," culturally elaborated by males. The same happened to young women. A man was totally "virile" (both in the worst and in the best sense of the word) and a woman, at the same time, was totally feminine. The relation between sexes was ruled by an old popular "particularistic" culture-code that was perfectly "separated" by bourgeois culture: or, to put it better, in a state of total extraneousness to it.

Consumerist society's power revolutionized in a few years this kind of life. It offered and imposed cultural "models" that already have popular ones. Tolerance (given and guided from above) made male-only and female-only no longer exist: the neighborhood's full of mixed groups, the gardens full of couples kissing. Young women go back home later in the evening and many of them are sexually very free. In each block there's at least one minor girl who makes love indiscriminately with all peer boys. The education aimed at the fulfilment of the popular "model" doesn't occur anymore for a male through his friends. He has to realize a "bourgeois" model (the petty consumerism of the outer suburb), and he's guided toward such a model form by girls. Because it's with girls that he spends most of his free time. The girls, who traditionally—this was, until now, the reality—have been the depositaries of normality and conformism, are today the depositaries of the new petty-bourgeois morality, which is tolerant but much more rigidly conformist. It's in the young women that the ideal of consumerism, as social success, finds a concrete life. It's in these women that a definitely free premarital eroticism finds a certain regulation, silently stipulated and approved. And all this is happening without any cultural support, without any cultural background.

The feminization of young men and the masculinization of young women is happening totally outside the culture of the truly lived life. This is making the boy strongly neurotic, because he's lost his old virile "model," and he's the one who's sexually afraid that he falls short of those freedoms he's been given, which are normalized and acted out by the girl. Obviously, the girl is made less neurotic; on the contrary she's living a moment of improvement and liberation. She's beginning to enjoy her life fully. But she risks becoming an "automaton" of such a freedom (which, I repeat, is always accorded from above). Her influence on the boy, already so powerful, is, for this lack of cultural conscience, totally negative: comradeship between sexes is a kind of neurotic obsessive complicity. These are the problems that confront young women.

My little girls, not my women. Dacia's "good women" are a petition of principle, as is the "wicked male." The survival of women belonging to the repressive traditional world (the women we find in the second part of the book) imposes a "cancelled fight." Instead this doesn't happen to the very young women. Young girls obtained Civil Rights. It's useless to stir up and fanaticize them to obtain some rights that they essentially already enjoy. What we need to do is to go and tell them "how" to exercise those rights: we have to submit them not to behavioral but cultural questions. Real problems always begin after rights are given (as African-American history teaches us): and this already happens when such rights have been obtained through a difficult and conscious fight, even more when they've been given real impulse—or because of the series of inevitable consequences of a more general fight—by Power.

1974. Translated by Giada Diano

LUTHERAN LETTER TO ITALO CALVINO

You say (*Corriere della Sera*, October 8, 1975): "Many people are responsible for the Circeo massacre[1] and they behave as if what they did were absolutely normal, just as if behind them they had an environment that understands and admires them."

But why is this?

You say: "In contemporary Rome what drives one crazy is that these monstrous events happen in a climate of absolute permissiveness, without even the shadow of a challenge to the repressive constrictions. . . ."

But why is this?

You say: ". . . the true danger comes from the presence of cancerous layers in our society. . . ."

But why is this?

You say: "There is only one step from moral social instability and from the social irresponsibility (*of a part of the Italian bourgeoisie, you say*) to the practice of torture and massacre. . . ."

But why is this?

You say: "We live in a world where the escalation in massacres and in the humiliation of the person are among the most visible signs of the historical change (where *political criminality and sexual criminality seem in this case reductive and optimistic definitions*, you say)."

But why is this?

You say: "The Nazis can be largely surpassed in cruelty at any moment."

But why is this?

---

1. Shocking murder in which two women were killed.

161

You say: "In other countries the crisis is the same, but it plays out within a society that is more solid."

But why is this?

It has been more than two years that I've tried to explain and vulgarize these "whys." And I'm finally outraged about the silence that's always surrounded me. A trial's been made over my indemonstrable Catholic *repression*. Nobody intervened to help me go on and go deeper in my attempts at explanation. Now, it's *silence* that's Catholic. For example, the silence of Giuseppe Branca, of Livio Zanetti, of Giorgio Bocca, of Claudio Petruccioli, of Alberto Moravia,[2] whom I had invited to intervene in a trial proposal of mine against the people guilty of this Italian condition that you describe with such apocalyptic anxiety—you, the sober one. And also your silence to my many public letters is Catholic. And also the silence of the leftist Catholics is Catholic (they should finally have the courage to define themselves as reformists or, with a bit more courage, Lutherans. After three centuries it's about time).

Let me tell you that he who speaks and tries to give explanations while surrounded by silence isn't Catholic. I couldn't shut up, like you're able to do now. "You have to have spoken a lot in order to be able to be silent" (a Chinese historian wonderfully says). So speak for once. Why?

You wrote a "notebook of grievances" in which you put together facts and phenomena to which you don't give any explanation, just like Lietta Tornabuoni[3] would, or a TV journalist, even if he or she is outraged.

---

2. Branca, Zanetti, Bocca, Petrucioli, and Moravia were writers and intellectuals, Alberto Moravia (1907–1990) being a close friend of Pasolini.

3. Tornabuoni, an Italican film critic.

Why?

But I've something to say also about your "notebook," beyond the lack of "whys."

I've something to say about the fact that you create scapegoats that are: "part of the bourgeoisie," "Rome," the "neofascists."

It seems evident from this that you lean on certitudes that were valued *before*. The certitudes (as I was saying to you in another letter) that comforted and even gratified us in a cleric-fascist context. The secular, rational, democratic, progressive certitudes. The way they are now, they're no longer of value. The historical change already happened, and those certitudes remained as they were.

To still speak of "part of the bourgeoisie" as guilty is an old and mechanical discourse, because the bourgeoisie today is at the same time *worse* than 10 years ago, and *better*. All of it. Including the one of Parioli or San Babila.[4] To say to you why it's worse (violence, aggressiveness, dissociation from the *other*, racism, vulgarity, brutal hedonism), but also to say why it's better (a certain laicism, a certain acceptance of values that used to belong to few people, the vote at the referendum, June 15th's vote) is useless.

To speak of the city of Rome as guilty is like going all the way back to the most pure Fifties, when people from Torino and Milan (and Friuli) considered Rome the center of every corruption: with clear and open racist manifestations. Rome with its Parioli today isn't worse than Milan with its San Babila, or Torino.

As far as the neo-fascists (youngsters), you realized that their definition has to be immensely enlarged, and the potential

---

4. Parioli is a bourgeois area in Rome, San Babila the same in Milan.

Nazi cruelty of which you talk (and of which from time to time I also talk) doesn't concern only them.

I have something to say also about another point of the "notebook without whys."

You have privileged the neo-fascists from the Parioli neighborhood with your interest and your indignation, because *they are bourgeois*. Their criminality interests you because it deals with the new sons of the bourgeoisie. You bring them from the truculent darkness of the news to the light of intellectual interpretation because their social class expects it. You behaved—it seems to me—like all the Italian press; in the Circeo murders the press sees a case that deals with bourgeoises, a case, I repeat, privileged. If the "poor" from the Roman slums or the poor who immigrated to Milan or Torino were doing the same thing, no one would have talked about it to that extent. Due to racism. Because the "poor" of the slums and the "poor" immigrants are considered criminals beforehand.

So, the poor of the Roman slums and the poor immigrants, meaning the youth of the lower classes, can do and *effectively do do* (as the news says with scary clarity) the same things that the Parioli youngsters did, and with the same spirit, the one that's the object of your "descriptiveness."

Every night the youngsters of the Roman borgate[5] have thousands of orgies (they call them "bashes") similar to those of Circeo; moreover, they're also drug addicts.

The murder of Rosaria Lopez was probably a second-degree murder (something that I don't consider at all a mitigating circumstance): every evening those hundreds of "bashes" imply a rough sadistic ceremonial.

---

5. A "borgata" (plural: "borgate") is a working-class suburb or village within Rome.

The impunity all these years of the criminal bourgeois and in particular of the neo-fascists has nothing to envy with the impunity of the slum criminals. (The Carlino brothers[6] of Torpignattara were enjoying the same conditional discharge as the "Pariolini"). Impunity miraculously concluded, partially with June 15th.

What can we get from all of this? That the "gangrene" doesn't spread only in certain layers of the bourgeois—Roman; neo-fascist—infecting the country and thus the people of the lower classes, but that there's a source of corruption that's far more distant and total. And here I'm repeating the litany.

The "production mode" has changed (enormous quantity, superfluous goods, hedonist function). But production doesn't produce only goods, it produces along with them social relationships, humanity. Thus the "new mode of production" produced a new humanity, meaning a "new culture," modifying the human being (in this particular case, the Italian) anthropologically. This "new culture" cynically destroyed the pre-existing cultures (genocide), from the traditional bourgeoisie to the various pluralistic popular cultures. For the models and values that it destroys, this new culture substitutes new models and its own values (not yet defined and named): they are those of a new species of bourgeoisie. The sons of the bourgeoisie are thus privileged in accomplishing these new values, and in doing so (with incertitude and thus aggressiveness), they set themselves up as examples to those who economically aren't capable of doing it, and they are reduced to sham and ferocious imitators. From there, their killer nature is SS-like. The phenomenon concerns the whole country. And the "whys" are there and are quite

6. Peter and Sam Carlino, noted mafia bosses who ended up in the United States.

clear. Clarity that, I admit, doesn't appear in this piece, which I'm writing here like a telegram. But you know very well how to get information, if you want to respond, discuss, reply. Something that I finally expect you to do.

Note: Politicians have difficulty recovering in such a project. There's a fight for survival. Every day they have to find a handle to remain attached to the place where they fight (for themselves; the others are not important). The press accurately mirrors their chaotic everyday life, the vortices in which they're trapped and swept away. And it mirrors also the magic words, or pure verbalism, to which they're attached, reducing real political perspectives to that. The journalists that are the authors of such a mirroring process seem to be accomplices of this pure everyday life, mythologized (as the "practice") because "serious." Maneuvers, conjurations, intrigues, put-up jobs of the Palace are passed off as serious events. While for someone who has no special interests, these are nothing else than tragicomic contortions and, naturally, sly and unworthy.

Union members can't help anymore. Lama, whom all the opinion makers had the habit of crawling up to, like crying puppies under a dog, couldn't tell us anything. He's the equal and opposite, meaning opposite and equal, to Moro,[7] with whom he deals. The reality and perspectives are verbal: what counts is the "thrown-together present." It isn't important that Lama is forced to do this, while the Christian Democrats live this. Today it seems that only platonic intellectuals (I add: Marxists)—maybe without any information, but certainly without special interests and complicity—have the possibility of foreseeing what's really

---

7. Aldo Moro (1916–1978), leader of Democratic Christians Party and two-time premier of Italy; he was kidnapped and killed by the Red Brigade.

happening: of course with the understanding that this intuition would be translated—literally translated—by scientists, also platonic, in terms of the only science in which reality is objectively certain, like the one of Nature, that is Political Economy.

1975. Translated by Flavio Rizzo

MARIANNE MOORE, *THE PLUMED BASILISK*

The Flowers of Evil was published in 1857 and, as is well known, it turned all of Italian literature old and downsized it to a state of pure provincial marginality in one shot. This state of inferiority of Italian literature, compared with the most important European literatures, lasted a century, and it's not yet really over.

A *florilegium* of the *Flowers* opens an anthology published by Mondadori that contains 21 poets, both Italian and foreign. *Flowers* is translated, to tell the truth not very well, by Giovanni Raboni, as it seems clear he doesn't like the marble-like and perfect surface of the Baudelarian disease. Then an aphonic and coquettish Umberto Saba, with some quite bookish "haiku" from the Twenties, appears. As far as I'm concerned, I didn't feel the necessity of a reordered rereading of this small section of *Songbook*. I'm not saying it—as I won't say of the rest—to hammer the book by Mondadori, edited by Forti and Pontiggia. It's a document; I don't think it intends to "impose" values. Even Dylan Thomas has here a few unpublished pieces or unknown poems that don't add much to his stature: actually, they impoverish him, unraveling a bit his game of automatic monologues and of his furious creativity, both venerable and scornful. The poems of Rene Daumal, a poet who worked along with the Surrealists during the Twenties and the Thirties, are also a disappointment, Also disappointing are all the other foreign poets, from Octavio Paz to Yves Bonnefoy, from the poets of the New York School (except Ashbery) to the empty Ted Hughes, the boring spiritualism of the Latinos, and the Pound reduced to quotations of casual and amateurish readings (with a bit of ancient languages) in Anglo-Saxon.

The Italians Garboli and Davico Bonino safeguard themselves, joking (even if Garboli's joke leads to a very painful game with its attempt to bring back to life someone between Noventa and Soldati, he does that with the fascination of Bassani's "sublime"). Antonio Porta seems completely emptied. The rest of them are unimportant, as well as that Eros Alesi about whom a simple life document is presented (he died in a madhouse when he was 20 years old after a trip to India, drug addicted along with his Piazza Bologna sad girlfriend). He was from Ciampino. His father was a jockey and used to get drunk and abuse his mother. This is the starting point of the usual tragedy that more or less we all lived. The only difference is that in these years fashion's insisted that this tragedy be intolerable and emphatic, and has wanted extreme remedies. I have no particular pity for this poor kid, weak and not well read, who died for the same reason one lets his hair grow long. The less rights one has, the greater the freedom. The real slavery of the Black Americans started the day they got their Civil Rights. Tolerance is the worst repression. It's tolerance that decided the fashion of drugs, of death and the extremist revolt. The weakest fell for it, with the presumption of being champions. In reality they've been champions of the most unforgiving conformism.

Among the Italians who are far better than the others there's Domenico Naldini, with a few small poems that also have been written as a joke, and with that delightful touch that Sandro Penna by now has already consumed completely, leaving to Naldini the bitter dregs; and Andrea Zanzotto offers us an extraordinary piece (he's been doing that for a few years now) this time around, about the Pasqua di Maggio, meaning about an Easter that never arrives. Here finally Pound is a reference to highest culture. His vatic delirium is full of real cultural interests, from ethnology to agriculture, from the history of religions (the egg symbol—eternal return) to medicine. It's a rustic and drunken poetry, where the cosmic is assured by an intellectual strength used comically.

The dialect poet Franco Loi remains a bit off to the side (he writes in Milanese slang he's of Sardinian origin), but the Italian translation is better than the original text. The translation, while flirting with the impossibility of translating the untranslatable, in reality flatters untranslatability, and it allows us to have a glimpse of rare and buried beauties in the text, enjoyed by others and elsewhere—an operation that's not banal, but rather quite skillful. About Fernando Camon (also with linguistic poverty, almost dialect), I won't speak, out of discretion, being myself the person who introduces him.

John Ashbery, the best, as I said, of the New York School— a humble Poundian who talks about drugs and the fashionable existential extremism—is translated by Silvano Sabbadini, the same who translated the whole of Olson's book, *The Maximus Poems*. But even Olson is a disappointment. He is a simple Poundian. The introductions talk about the New York School like an "event" that happens on the page, which as such is the "arena" of such an event, leaving the reader confused, guilty, and with the impression of being a poor devil surpassed by time. While talking about Olson and the Black Mountain Group to which he belongs, the introductions talk about "dynamic and structural function in the *field* of the page," that substitutes the old rhythmic unity of verse and of stanza, so that poetry organizes itself as an "organic space." Words that are absolutely without any sense. In fact both Ashbery and Olson are, I repeat, epigones of Pound, common neurotics rather than crazies. The Poundian chat is Homeric, and his artifact hermeneutics grandly include characters that are almost possessed, in their daily life, by a cosmic linguistic mania. They inhabit the small American and Pisan world as immense ghosts whose voices pour over the globe. The small characters of Olson, through whom he also monologues while chatting, are provincial and folkloristic, and they remain so. Existence, as shapeless totality, is replaced by sociology, very modestly. The humor with which—conventionally—Olson corrects his mythology, in reality has nothing to minimize: the mythic world of Olson is already minimum.

Amid Zanzotto, and that Naldini who seems like he doesn't dare to even exist, the best choice is Auden. His are the best verses of the book (that stupendous final piece of *City Without Walls*). There is also a poem of his dedicated to Marianne Moore, on the occasion of her 80th birthday, November 15, 1967. Marianne Moore died five years later in New York City. In these months the volume of all her poems came out in Italy, *The Plumed Basilisk*, which starts with the *Selected Poems* of 1935 and ends with *Collected Later* in 1951.

What a marvelous reading, this *Plumed Basilisk*! It puts itself unexpectedly among the fundamental readings of my life (if that's of any interest), from the ancient readings of the Greek Cantos, Rimbaud, Machado, to the most recent Mandelstam and the last Bertolucci. I consider it great luck to have reserved this reading for today (I only knew a few things by Marianne Moore, quoted or put into anthologies): I've had the happiness of a teenager. When we like a book to this extent, it's difficult, actually impossible, to come up with a critical discourse right away: it seems, irrationally, even a sacrilege. I'm counting on the fact that my reader will take my word on this.

The Jerboa, The Pangolin, The Plumed Basilisk, and let's add also *A Carriage from Sweden*, are poems to learn by heart. It's to learn by heart for example:

"Repeated / evidence has proved that it can live /
on what can not revive / its youth. The sea grows old in it.";

"If ardor could be exchanged for avidity, / if heat can seem fury, / finished plots are not permitted";

"A very strict emsplendorphasis on this or that / quality disturbs our pleasure";

"Connected to the splendor / of the hard majesty of sophistication that is superior to opportunity, / these are rich instruments on which to experiment. / But why dissect destiny with instruments / even more specialized than the elements of destiny itself?";

"The passion for straightening up one's neighbor is in itself a grievous sickness, / better, repugnance that in itself makes no claim to merit";

"An aspect may deceive; as the / elephant's columbine-tubed trunk / held waveringly out— / an at will heavy thing—is / delicate. / Art is unfortunate.";

"Whoever again / and again says, 'I'll never give in,' never sees / that you're not free / until you've been made captive by / supreme belief . . .";

"With the Socrates of / animals as with Sophocles the Bee, on whose / tombstone a hive was incised, sweetness tinctures / his gravity.";

"Unconfusion submits / its confusion to proof; it's / not a Herod's oath that cannot change.";

and finally the confession of a moralist that fakes an aristocratic moralism:

". . . he was one who told us things / that would never have been able to be actualized / and his stories were better than all the un-chummy, senile rigmarole that is spoken with oh such certainty. . . ."

But in reality, all of this is told almost by chance because it's learned from life, one learns one thing, another another, with the difference, also unimportant, that one takes "Herod's oaths," and another doesn't. Moreover discretion requires that everything is worth another thing. There's nothing to teach; the real scholar "finds in his opinion his peace" and doesn't want anything else from himself or others. What counts is to narrate: it's ecstasy that gives inspiration, and convenience that gives form. Narrating about what? It's enough to read an encyclopedia, or an ornithology book, or one on botany: there's no limit to themes, just as there's no gradualism in being. It's vitality—left partially unconscious ("There's a strong dose of poetry in unconscious / meticulousness"; "Their whole dignity was . . . in caring, not in madness")—partially translated in the highest quality of culture, which goes wild in the immense reservations of solitude.

1973. Translated by Flavio Rizzo

POEMS 1964–1971

TO CONTEMPORARY LITERATI

I see you, you exist, we continue being friends
    happy to see and greet one another in some café
or in the homes of ironical Roman ladies.
    But our greetings, our smiles, our mutual passions
are acts in a no man's land . . . a wasteland
    for you, a border for me between one history and the other.
We can't really have any rapport anymore, I fear,
    but it's what's in us that makes the world its own enemy.

1958–59. Translated by Jack Hirschman

FRAGMENT TO DEATH

I come to you and return to you,
sentiment born of light, of heat,
baptized when the beginning was joy,
recognized in Pier Paolo
at the origin of a craving epopeia:
I've walked in the light of history,
but my being was always heroic
under your dominion, intimate thought.
Every real act of the world, of history,
coagulated in the stream of light,
in the atrocious distrust of your flame:
and it was wholly verified within it,
losing its life in order to regain it:
and life was real only if beautiful . . .

The fury of confession first,
then the fury of clarity:
it was from you that it was born,
hypocrite, obscure sentiment! And now,
let them accuse my every passion,
let them sling mud, call me deformed, impure,
obsessed, amateur, perjurer:
you isolate me, you give me the certainty of life:
I'm on the pyre, I play the card of fire
and I win this little immense good
I have, I win this infinite,
miserable compassion of mine

that makes even righteous anger my friend:
I can do so, because I've suffered you so!

I return to you, like an emigrant
returns to his country and re-discovers it:
I've done well (with my intellect)
and I'm happy, just like
I used to be, destitute as always.
A black rage of poetry in my chest.
A crazy young man's old age.
Once your joy was confused
with terror, it's true, and now
almost with other joy,
livid, arid: my disappointed passion.
You really frighten me now,
because you are really close, included
in my state of rage, of obscure
fame, in the anxiety of a newly born creature.

I am sane, if you like,
the neurosis branches out beside me,
exhaustion desiccates me, but
it doesn't have me: at my side
the last light of youth is laughing.
At this point, I've had all that I wanted:
I've actually even gone beyond
certain hopes the world had: emptied,
there you are, inside me,
filling my time and all times.
I've been rational and I've been

irrational: to the very end.
And now . . . ah, the desert, deafened
by the wind, the stupendous and other-worldly
sun of Africa that illuminates the world.

Africa! My one and only
alternative . . . .

1960. Translated by Pasquale Verdicchio

THE RAGE

I go to the gate of the garden, a sunken
little passageway of stone at ground
level, across from the suburban
orchard that's been there since the days of Mameli,[1]
with its pines, its roses, its radishes.
Looking around, behind this paradise of village
tranquility, we see the yellow facades of the fascist
skyscrapers from the latest spate of buildings,
and looking lower, beyond some thick plates of glass
there's a shed, sepulchral. Drowsing
in full sunlight, a bit chilly, is the grand orchard
with the little white nineteenth-century house
in the center, where Mameli lies dead,
and a blackbird's singing, weaving his web of intrigue.

This poor garden of mine, all
of stone . . . But I've bought an oleander
—the new pride of my mother—
and vases of every kind of flower,
and a wooden frying-pan, an obedient,
rosy and malicious little Cupid statue
found at Porta Portese when looking for furniture for
                      the new house. Colors?
A few, the season's still so young: gold
splashes of light, and greens, all the greens . . .

---

1. Poet and general who died in 1849. The "Hymn of Mameli" is the national an-
them of Italy.

Just a bit of red, menacing and splendid,
half-hidden, dour and without joy,
a rose. It hangs without fanfare
on the adolescent branch, as if gazing out of a spy-hole,
a shy remnant of a paradise in pieces.

Nearby, and even more self-effacing, it seems we have
a poor thing, defenseless and naked,
a pure whim
of nature, who found herself in the air and the sunlight
alive but in a way that awes and humbles her
and makes her almost ashamed
to be so brazen
in her stark delicacy as a flower.
I get even closer and I smell her . . .

Ah! Shouting doesn't say it and silence is no better:
nothing can express a whole existence!
I reject any attempt at it . . . I only know
that in this rose I could breathe,
in one single miserable instant,
the smell of my life, the smell of my mother . . .

So why don't I react, why not tremble
with joy or exult in the pure anguish of it?
Why don't I hail
this ancient knot of my existence?
I know why: because the demon of rage is locked
up in me by now. A small, mute, dark
feeling that intoxicates me:
an exhausting, they say, feverish impatience

in the nerves: but my mind's no longer free.
The pain it gives me little by little alienates me
from myself so I just abandon myself
it takes on a life of its own, whirling around
as it wills while my pulse goes out of control
in my temples, my heart fills with pus,
I'm no longer master of my life.

Once, nothing could have beaten me.
I was cloistered in my life as in the maternal
womb, in that warm
smell of that simple wet rose.
But I fought to leave it behind, that provincial
countryside life, a twenty-year-old poet, always always
suffering desperately
and as desperately feeling joy . . . The battle ended
in victory. My private life's
no longer closed up within petals of a rose,
—a house, a mother, an exhausting passion.
It's public. But also the world which had been unknown
to me is now ordinary, familiar,
has become known and, little by little,
is now a brutal, necessary duty.

I can't pretend now that I don't know the world,
or that I don't know how it wants me.
What type of love
are we talking about here, what sleazy deal.
Not a single flame burns in this inferno
of unfeeling, and this dry fury
that stops my heart

from responding to a smell is a cheap excuse
for passion . . . Almost forty years old
I find myself in a rage, like a young guy
who knows nothing of himself except that he's young,
and he goes to battle against the old world.
And like a young guy, without pity
or restraint, I don't hide
this state I'm in: I'll never have peace, never.

1960. Translated by Jonathan Richman

FRAGMENTS FROM A 1961 DIARY

I know, because I wake up with so much strength in my head:
the strength to suck up the new, sweet
power of daylight woken ahead of me,
and to express the absolute, already attained in secret and
in peace, with the most naked words: it's grief, my pain that
always has a reason, is never without an object,
is not neuroses: it's anger, disappointment,
it's fear, it's fury that physically
bleeds in my chest and throat.
Ah, morning! I know it, it's summertime, steady
as a sea, in its freshness
the city's ready for an entire day,
and its noises are sheer and deeply grieving
like human beings become cool
doves, gentle elephants . . . animals in life . . .

July 31, 1961

My "youth" has lasted too long.
The mayor of Sansepolcro writes me
—herr professor, communist—that I am
a "hope." No, I'm not a hope.
I'm (and do I know it!) a reality:
a reality gone beyond itself,
turned toward itself like a monster.
I see it come to the surface these days
that I'm with the young people, only them:
days of a destruction of every life,

stupendous as every destruction
because only at the end is there hope.

Summer 1961

There's something (since everything ends up
with being only something
in us, who are flesh and imagination)
that's a rational idea of the world.
I live by it, I will live by it. This something
is the extension of my life.
But this something floats
upon another something: that something
that came only from my adolescence:

a triumphant sense of death,
of a terrific aesthetic uselessness . . .
I was scared of it then: it was delicate
to touch it because it was everything. And then
since it was only aesthetic (it had only
beauty to exist for)
a single instant of ugliness
would have twisted it frightfully.
Now I can allow myself less exquisite mystery.
Like a good gravy, a serious aestheticism
toward death can season the truth.

Summer 1961.

Translated by Jack Hirschman

THE BEAUTIFUL BANNERS

Morning dreams, when the sun
already rules
with a ripeness
only the peddler knows,
who's been walking the streets for hours
with the beard of a sick man
over the wrinkles of his poor youth;
when the sun rules
over realms of already warm vegetables, over
weary awnings, over the masses
whose clothes already are darkening with poverty
—and of course hundreds of trolleys are coming and going
along avenue tracks that encircle the inexpressibly
sweet-smelling city;

Ten-in-the-morning dreams
of a man sleeping alone like a pilgrim in his doghouse,
an unidentified corpse
—they appear in lucid Greek characters
and, in the simple holiness of two or three syllables,
pregnant precisely with the whiteness of the triumphant sun—
they foretell a reality matured in the depths and now ripe as
        the sun,
to be enjoyed or to be feared.

 What's the morning dream telling me of?
        "the sea, with slow grandiose waves of blue grain,

plunges downward working with an irreducible uterine
    fury

and almost happy—because in giving joy
it also verifies the cruelest act of fate—
it pounds your island which by now
is reduced to a few feet of land."

Help, loneliness is coming on.

Never mind that I know I've willed it like a king.
In sleep, inside me, there's a silent scared kid
begging forgiveness, anxiously running for shelter
with an agitation that "reveals virtue"—poor thing.
The idea of
being alone terrifies him
like a corpse in the depths of the earth.

So long, Dignity, in dreams or in the morning as well.
Whoever has to cry, cries:
Whoever has to grab hold of someone's coattails;
grabs hold and yanks and yanks at them
so that those mud-colored faces turn
and look at him in his terrorized eyes
and are pervaded by his tragedy
and understand just how awful his state of being is!

The whiteness of the sun on everything
like a ghost that history
presses on the eyelids
with the weight of baroque or Romanesque marble . . .

I've willed my loneliness.
through a monstrous process
that could only perhaps reveal
a dream created inside a dream . . .

Meanwhile I'm alone.
Lost in the past.
(Because a guy has only that period in his life).

All of a sudden my poet friends,
who shared with me
the holy whiteness of the Sixties,
men and women just a bit older
or a bit younger, are there in the sunlight.

I didn't have the grace
to hold them close to me—in the shadow of a life
that unfolds too attached
to the radical sloth of my soul.

Age, that is, has made
two masks
of my mother and me
that have nevertheless lost nothing
of morning tenderness
—and the ancient performance
is repeated
with an authenticity
that only dreaming within a dream
I could perhaps call by its name.

The whole world's my unburied body.
An atoll crumbled
by the lashes of the blue grains of the sea.

What to do at the wake if not get some dignity?
And, what's more, maybe a bit of exile-time:
the time when an Ancient would have given reality
to reality
and the loneliness ripened around him
would have had loneliness' shape.

Instead, as in dream,
I keep painfully trying to give myself illusions
of an earthworm paralyzed by incomprehensible forces.
"But no! no! it's only a dream!
Reality
Is outside, in the triumphant sunlight,
on the avenues and in empty cafés,
in the supreme voicelessness of ten-in-the-morning,
a day like all the others, with its cross!"

My friend with his pope's chin, my
friend with the light-brown eyes . . .
My dear buddies from the North
rooted in elective affinities sweet as life
—they're there, in the sunlight.

Elsa as well, with her blond sorrow,
she—wounded, fallen, bleeding steed—
is there.

And my mother's close to me . . . but beyond any limit of time:
we're a couple of survivors in one.
Her sighs here in the kitchen,
her getting sick at the least hint of degrading scandal,
at the least suspicion that the hatred of that bunch
of sneering students under the room where I'm agonizing
will start up again—such things are
nothing but make my loneliness natural.

Like a wife put to the stake with the king
or buried with him
in a tomb that floats away like a skiff
toward the millennia—the faith of the Fifties
is here with me, already a little bit beyond the limits of time,
letting itself be pounded as well
by the furious patience of the blue grains of the sea.
And . . .
My loves of sheer sensuality
replicated in the sacred valleys of lust,
sadistic, masochistic, the pants
with their warm sacs
where a man's fate is outlined
—are acts I've performed alone
in the midst of a stupendously convulsive sea.

Slowly slowly thousands of holy gropes,
my hand on the warm swelling,
the kisses each time on a different
ever-more virginal mouth,
Ever nearer the enchantment of the species,
the principle that makes tender fathers of sons.

Slowly slowly
they've become stone monuments
that crowd my loneliness by the thousands.

Waiting
for a new wave of rationality
or a dream made in the depths of dreaming, to talk about
  them.

So I wake
once again
and dress and sit at my work table.
The light of the sun already is overripe,
the peddlers further away,
the vegetable warmth more acrid in the world's markets
along inexpressibly sweet-smelling avenues,
at the edge of sea, at the feet of volcanoes.
The whole world's at work on its future epoch.

Ah! The beautiful banners of the Forties!
A pretext for a clown to weep.

But that "white" something
in Greek letters
which the dream expert irrevocably showed me
sticks to me, dressed
at the work table.
Marble, wax, or lime
on my eyelids, at the corners of my eyes:
the joyously Romanesque,
hopelessly baroque whiteness of the sun in sleep.

Real sunlight was of that whiteness
and so were the factory walls
as well as
the dust itself (on dry afternoons when
the day before was a bit rainy):
the woolen rags, the rumpled grey jackets
and frayed pants of the workers
who'd still have been able to be partisans
were of that whiteness,
as was the heat of the new springtime
oppressed by the memory of other springtimes
buried for centuries
in those very same suburbs and villages
—and ready, God,
ready to be born again
on those little walls, on those streets.

On those little walls, on those streets
steeped in strange fragrance
where the red apples and cherries flourished
in the warmth, and their red color
had a burnish to it, as
if it had been immersed in the air of a hot storm,
a red almost brown, cherries like prunes,
little apples like plums that peeped out
among the browns, intense
weft of foliage, calm, springtime was
almost in no rush,
wanted to enjoy that warmth in which the world whispered,
in its old hope, passionately of a new hope.

And over all, the waving,
the humble sluggish waving
of the red banners. God! the beautiful banners
of the Forties!
waving one after another in a mass of poor
cloth, reddening, a true red
that broke through with the dazzling destitution
of the silk covers, or the clean linen of worker families
—and with the fire of the cherries, of the apples, violet
because of the dampness, bloody because a bit of sunlight
    struck it,
fiery red bunched together and trembling
in the heroic tenderness of an immortal season.

1962. Translated by Jack Hirschman

MONOLOGUE ON THE JEWS

How strange that I have a "sense of the eternal"
tonight.

    Have I maybe
gone back 20 years? I'm no longer
20 years old, so how

    can I see
people in glass cases—in the dust-clouds
of the millennia?

A night that touches all casual living
existence with its chill,
a few chests and mouths
among the billions that lived and died.

A horizon of dust-clouds,
with little weary bones,
vast deposits of personal deaths
or slaughters . . .

    No, I don't think
about Buchenwald, though . . .
the idea of so much stinking death

is the ground of my vision
of the world: the hollow cheeks,

the hair stuck to living skulls,
the flaccid shanks entangled
in revolting intimacy with other
shanks covered in rags; ribs
on display with ridiculous patience
in the light of an old Chaplin tragedy.

It happened like that!

    It's so exhausting
learning life's expressions—
the words, the idea of one's self,
courage, intelligence . . .

Even the healthiest of sons
seems to work so hard at resisting
the uncertainty of being a flower

of youth—even the most
fortunate, with all of youth's
gifts . . . Curls, a smile,

the kind brutality in his pants:
it takes so much hard work . . . costs
so many humiliations . . .

So instead one learned pretty early
to be a dead man.

    The photographs
are quiet testimonies:

in Buchenwald, look at them; if alive,
they haven't yet completely learned
life:

one of them still has the courage
to smile. Look at him,
the stinking little Jew

reduced to a skeleton in a stench of shit,
leaning indecently against his comrades
in agony, who still looks
at the camera and wears a smile!

He still hasn't learned the horror,
still hasn't learned the taste
of being martyred, the shudder
of the executioner who kills him en masse,

the exalting tremor of sex
in being killed as if he never were
a man: in genitally feeling
the voluptuousness of being naturally abject.

And the sons? They believed, they did,
it was an adult thing:
and look at them, how wise and absorbed they are.

Look at them, if you still live.

Spectral
little faces, unburied kittens

—but uncertain, even they,
about the past and the future.

The house in Bohemia or Lombardia,
the piano, the garden with magnolias,
the obscure Apocalypse.

You'll be born into a different family and uncertainty will be
your bread.

You'll have a life of ideals consecrated by your mother
in a nostalgia for rules and the norm will be your bread.

You'll contemplate a world ruled by a delicate morality
and delicacy will be your bread.

Eating that bread they died.

Look at them, if dead.
No longer is there a gesture of uncertainty:
each one immediately knows how things stand.

In a moment he unlearns the life
that was so much his, and learns
the death belonging supremely to others.

Ah, the photographs by this time
have freed every doubt about that.
The Jew alive in Buchenwald,

a nice bourgeois, still doesn't
know what the bourgeoisie is,
and wears a smile—horrible.

In death, on the contrary, he keeps
a conscious and pure secret:
the hollow cheeks, the hair

stuck like wretched wool
to his skull, the crab shanks
with big knees,

here's how one is, how one stands.
Then, at last, they speak;
rather, they sing. And the song

spreads throughout the world.

Uselessly, however, because the world's
died in its way and is already
chockablock with songs of death!

These death-songs I hear
returning home talking to myself
on this night when I'm no longer 20 years old.

Here—I tell myself—I've already written lines
but not as a monologue . . . It was a song, it was
a poor song, even mine!

Of someone alive, ay, not of someone dead!

Against the Swastika,
the Government of my nation,
the Catholic Church,

so that they don't prevent, here
in the ghetto, those having to stay armed
to save

what the faith of the living people
should preserve
with its only truth!

Here's the black van overturned,
here's the peace that the pavements
and railroad tracks at night in shadow have

over the Tevere with its old plane-trees . . .
Around here, the groups of night-bird
witnesses, in the daylight already breathing . . .

As in the wing of a church,
one voice asks and another responds,
and I come to understand . . .

Invisible Jewish kids
have capsized
this impious van of the fascists,

and here insults have exploded, and fists
resonated, and reason has cried out
its rights against the madness.

What can now interrupt the song of the dead?

I who return from my night
given over to sex and thus defenseless,
through excess of itself, before the bone-yards of the earth,

rather than that sex and death
are a single brutal exaltation
of libidinal peace,

     I feel
sex and death suddenly freezing up.

Is it possible life has such power?

A dozen living Jewish kids
in June of 1962,
a year like a thousand others

surfacing in the dust-clouds,
have made a holy demonstration
of what the living understand.

However, in their thousands of doubts,
doubts about man and about the Jew,
—perhaps for their having been here

and not being lost any longer in Roman streets
in the coolness of the Ghetto—
with an insolent glory of being absent

they have in them the same certainty as the dead.

I know the softness that wounds them,
the terror that weighs on their healthy hearts,
the virility of their doubting.

I know what it means to be different,
marked by a delicate destiny,
lost in a sincere moral dedication.

I know what it means for a mother
who's not like other mothers,
so that the world around unfolds

like a party forever denied
the sons of the sons!

They have nothing, those invisible kids
gone out of the Ghetto in which for centuries
their otherness was fixed,

which makes them different in health and purity
from what a man ought to be.
Except that, in the flower

of their youth, there's a sadness,
and I know it well, that bewilders them.

But despite that, they weren't afraid!

Despite that, they didn't renounce
even the physical strength of the son!

Ah, never was an act of violence

more delicate, circumfused
with respect and nobility,
necessary and almost reluctant

to fulfill those exploits in which
one evening this summertime
those kids sacrificed delicacy

for their and the world's honor.

Taken away from my peace, in front of their Temple,
I lose myself in a virgin thought:
"Commit violence!"

You've been born to live frightened
by an overwhelming feeling of having
an undeserved existence.

You've been called blind, dumb, lame, possessed,
leprous, monstrous children because you've never
recognized the destitution of your fathers.

You've been fated to never know the nights in which
violent brothers, free from terror, sing and dance
in the heart of life.

Wretched Roman night
dominated by the peace of those who've already lived
—who are so very much

deprived—and this privation
turns into song, a dismal expanse of dust-clouds!
Maybe life will begin

when the angels of resignation
—the poor at heart, the meek, the vulnerable,
the wretches, the Jews, the Blacks,

the young, the inmates, the virgins,
the peasants, the people lost
in the innocence of the barbarity,

all those who live dedicated
in humiliating otherness—
will commit violence.

Then life will begin!

1963. Translated by Jack Hirschman

VICTORY

Where are the weapons?
I've only those of my reason
and in my violence there's no place

for even the trace of an act that's not
intellectual. Is it laughable
if, suggested by my dream on this

gray morning, which a dead man saw
and other dead men also will see
but for us is just another morning,

I scream words of struggle?
Who knows what will become of me
at noon, but the old poet is "ab joy"[1]

who speaks like a lark or a starling or
a young man longing for death.
Where are the weapons? The old days

will not return, I know; the red
Aprils of youth are gone.
Only a dream, of joy, can open

Note: The "day of victory" of the poem's last line is April 25, 1945, when German troops surrendered in Italy, effectively ending the Italian fascist era begun in the year of Pasolini's birth, 1922.

1. "Ab joy," Provençal for " joyous."

a season of armed pain.
I who was an unarmed Partisan,[2]
mystical, beardless, nameless,

now I sense in life the horribly
perfumed seed of the Resistance.
In the morning the leaves are still

as they once were on the Tagliamento
and Livenza[3]—it's not a storm coming
or the night falling. It's the absence

of life, contemplating itself,
distanced from itself, intent on
understanding those terrible yet serene

forces that still fill it—aroma of April!
an armed youth for each blade of grass,
each a volunteer longing to die.
. . . .
Good. I wake up and—for the first time
in my life—I want to take up arms.
Absurd to say it in poetry

—and to four friends from Rome, two from Parma
who will understand me in this nostalgia
ideally translated from the German, in this archaeological

---

2. Generic name for fighters who formed the Resistance to fascism during the war.
3. Rivers of Friuli, where Pasolini grew up.

calm, which contemplates a sunny, depopulated
Italy, home of barbaric Partisans who descend
the Alps and Apennines, down the ancient roads . . .

My fury comes only at dawn.
At noon I'll be with my countrymen
at work, at meals, at reality, which raises

the flag, white today, of General Destinies.
And you, communists, my comrades /non-comrades,
shadows of comrades, estranged first cousins

lost in the present as well as the distant,
unimagined days of the future, you, nameless
fathers who have heard calls that

I thought were like mine, which
burn now like fires abandoned
on cold plains, along sleeping

rivers, on bomb-quarried mountains. . . .
. . . .
I take upon myself all the blame (my old
vocation, unconfessed, easy work)
for our desperate weakness,

because of which millions of us,
all with a life in common, couldn't
persist to the end. It's over,

let's sing along, tralala. They're falling,
fewer and fewer, the last leaves of
the War and the martyred victory,

destroyed little by little by what
would become reality,
not only dear Reaction but also the birth of

beautiful social-democracy, tralala.

I take (with pleasure) on myself the guilt
for having left everything as it was:
for the defeat, for the distrust, for the dirty

hopes of the Bitter Years,[4] tralala.
And I'll take upon myself the tormenting
pain of the darkest nostalgia,

which summons up regretted things
with such truth as to almost
resurrect them or reconstruct the shattered

conditions that made them necessary (trallallallalla). . . .
. . . .
Where have the weapons gone, peaceful
productive Italy, you who have no importance in the world?
In this servile tranquility, which justifies

---

4. The years when fascism was dominant.

yesterday's boom, today's bust—from the sublime
to the ridiculous—and in the most perfect solitude,
j'accuse! Not, calm down, the Government or the Latifundia[5]

or the Monopolies—but rather their high priests,
Italy's intellectuals, all of them,
even those who rightly call themselves

my good friends. These must have been the worst
years of their lives, for having accepted
a reality that didn't exist. The result

of this conniving, of this embezzling of ideals,
is that the real reality now has no poets.
(I? I'm desiccated, obsolete.)

Now that Togliatti has exited amid
the echoes from the last bloody strikes,
old, in the company of the prophets,

who, alas, were right—I dream of weapons
hidden in the mud, the elegiac mud
where children play and old fathers toil—

while from the gravestones melancholy falls,
the lists of names crack,
the doors of the tombs explode,

---

5. Large landed property farms where workers toiled for slave wages.

and the young corpses in the overcoats
they wore in those years, the loose-fitting
trousers, the military cap on their Partisan

hair, descend, along the walls
where the markets stand, down the paths
that join the town's vegetable gardens

to the hillsides. They descend from their graves, young men
whose eyes hold something other than love:
a secret madness, of men who fight

as though called by a destiny different from their own.
With that secret that's no longer a secret,
they descend, silent, in the dawning sun,

and, though so close to death, theirs is the happy tread
of those who'll journey far in the world.
But they're the inhabitants of the mountains, of the wild

shores of the Po, of the remotest places
on the coldest plains. What are they doing here?
They've come back, and no one can stop them. They don't hide

their weapons, which they hold without grief or joy,
and no one looks at them, as though blinded by shame
at that obscene flashing of guns, at that tread of vultures

that descend to their obscure duty in the sunlight.
. . . .

Who has the courage to tell them
that the ideal secretly burning in their eyes
is finished, belongs to another time, that the children

of their brothers haven't fought for years,
and that a cruelly new history has produced
other ideals, quietly corrupting them? . . .

Rough like poor barbarians, they'll touch
the new things that in these two decades human
cruelty has procured, things incapable of moving

those who seek justice. . . .

But let's celebrate, let's open the bottles
of the good wine of the Cooperative. . . .
To always new victories, and new Bastilles!

Rafosco, Bacò[6]. . . . Long life!
To your health, old friend! Strength, comrade!
And best wishes to the beautiful party!

From beyond the vineyards, from beyond the farm ponds
comes the sun: from the empty graves,
from the white gravestones, from that distant time.

But now that they're here, violent, absurd,
with the strange voices of emigrants,
hanged from lampposts, strangled by garrotes,

---

6. Friulian wines.

who'll lead them in the new struggle?
Togliatti himself is finally old,
as he wanted to be all his life,

and he holds, alarmed in his breast,
like a pope, all the love we have for him,
though stunted by epic affection,

loyalty that accepts even the most inhuman
fruit of a scorched lucidity, tenacious as a scabie.
"All politics is Realpolitik," warring

soul, with your delicate anger!
You don't recognize a soul other than this one
which has all the prose of the clever man,

of the revolutionary devoted to the honest
common man (even the complicity
with the assassins of the Bitter Years grafted

onto protector classicism, which makes
the communist respectable): you don't recognize the heart
that becomes slave to its enemy, and goes

where the enemy goes, led by a history
that is the history of both, and makes them, deep down,
perversely, brothers; you don't recognize the fears

of a consciousness that, by struggling with the world,
shares the rules of the struggle over the centuries,
as through a pessimism into which hopes

drown to become more virile. Joyous
with a joy that knows no hidden agenda,
this army—blind in the blind

sunlight—of dead young men comes
and waits. If their father, their leader, absorbed
in a mysterious debate with Power and bound

by its dialectics, which history renews ceaselessly—
if he abandons them,
in the white mountains, on the serene plains,

little by little in the barbaric breasts
of the sons, hate becomes love of hate,
burning only in them, the few, the chosen.

Ah, Desperation that knows no laws!
Ah, Anarchy, free love
of Holiness, with your valiant songs!
. . . .
I take also upon myself the guilt for trying
betraying, for struggling surrendering,
for accepting the good as the lesser evil,

symmetrical antinomies that I hold
in my fist like old habits. . . .
All the problems of man, with their awful statements

of ambiguity (the knot of solitudes
of the ego that feels itself dying
and doesn't want to come before God naked):

all this I take upon myself, so that I can understand,
from the inside, the fruit of this ambiguity:
a beloved man, in this uncalculated

April, from whom a thousand youths
fallen from the world beyond await, trusting, a sign
that has the force of a faith without pity,

to consecrate their humble rage.
Pining away within Nenni[7] is the uncertainty
with which he re-entered the game, and the skillful

coherence, the accepted greatness,
with which he renounced epic affection,
though his soul could claim title

to it: and, exiting a Brechtian stage
into the shadows of the backstage,
where he learns new words for reality, the uncertain

hero breaks at great cost to himself the chain
that bound him, like an old idol, to the people,
giving a new grief to his old age.

The young Cervis,[8] my brother Guido,
the young men of Reggio killed in 1960,[9]
with their chaste and strong and faithful

---

7. Pietro Nenni (1891–1980), head of the Italian Socialist Party.
8. The Cervis were brothers killed by the Nazis.
9. During riots in Reggio Emilia for better working conditions in 1960, several dem-
onstrators were killed.

eyes, source of the holy light,
look to him, and await his old words.
But, a hero by now divided, he lacks

by now a voice that touches the heart:
he appeals to the reason that's not reason,
to the sad sister of reason, which wants

to understand the reality within reality, with a passion
that refuses any extremism, any temerity.
What to say to them? That reality has a new tension,

which is what it is, and by now one has
no other course than to accept it. . . .
That the revolution becomes a desert

if it's always without victory . . . that it may not be
too late for those who want to win, but not with the violence
of the old, desperate weapons. . . .

That one must sacrifice coherence
to the incoherence of life, attempt a creator
dialogue, even if that goes against our conscience.

That the reality of even this small, stingy
State is greater than us, is always an awesome thing:
and one must be part of it, however bitter that is. . . .

But how do you expect them to be reasonable,
this band of anxious men who left—as
the songs say—home, bride,

life itself, specifically in the name of Reason?
. . . .

But there may be a part of Nenni's soul that wants
to say to these comrades—come from the world beyond,
in military clothes, with holes in the soles

of their bourgeois shoes, and their youth
innocently thirsting for blood—
to shout: "Where are the weapons? Come on, let's

go, get them, in the haystacks, in the earth,
don't you see that nothing's changed?
Those who were weeping still weep.

Those of you who have pure and innocent hearts,
go and speak in the Capernaums[10] of the slums,

in the Gomorrahs of the skyscrapers of the poor,
       who behind their walls and their alleys
hide the shameful plague, the passivity of those
who know they're cut off from the days of the future.

Those of you who have a heart
devoted to accursèd lucidity,
go into the factories and schools

to remind the people that nothing in these years has
changed the quality of knowing, eternal pretext,
sweet and useless form of Power, never of truth.

---

10. Actually the place where Christ lived and taught in a synagogue.

Those of you who obey an honest
old imperative of religion,
go among the children who grow

with hearts empty of real passion,
to remind them that the new evil
is still and always the division of the world. Finally,

those of you to whom a sad accident of birth
in families without hope gave the thick shoulders, the curly
hair of the criminal, dark cheekbones, eyes without pity—

go, to start with, to the Crespis, to the Agnellis,
to the Vallettas,[11] to the potentates of the companies
that brought Europe to the shores of the Po:

and for each of them comes the hour that has no
equal to what they have and what they hate.
Those who've stolen from the common good

precious capital and whom no law can
punish, well, then, go and tie them up with the rope
of massacres. At the end of the Piazzale Loreto[12]

there are still, repainted, a few
gas pumps, red in the quiet
sunlight of the springtime that returns

---

11. Names of big company owners.
12. Piazzale Loreto is the square in Milan where Mussolini's body was hung upside down.

with its destiny: It's time to make it a burial ground again!"
. . . .
They're leaving . . . Help! They're turning away,
their backs beneath the heroic coats
of beggars and deserters. . . . How serene are

the mountains they return to, so lightly
the submachine guns tap their hips, to the tread
of the sun setting on the intact

forms of life, which has become what it was before
to its very depths. Help, they're going away!—back to their
silent worlds in Marzabotto or Via Tasso. . . .[13]

With the broken head, our head, humble
treasure of the family, big head of the second-born,
my brother resumes his bloody sleep, alone

among the dried leaves, in the serene
retreats of a wood in the pre-Alps, lost in
the golden peace of an interminable Sunday. . . .
. . . .
And yet, this is a day of victory.

1964. Translated by Norman MacAfee
with Luciano Martinengo

---

13. Marzabotto was a village destroyed, along with its inhabitants, by the Nazis, and Via Tasso is a street in Rome where the Nazis and Fascists had their torture headquarters.

ONE OF MANY EPILOGUES

Hey, Ninarieddo,[1] do you recall that dream . . .
which we've spoken of so many times . . .
I was in a car driving alone with an empty
seat beside me, and you ran alongside
at the height of the still half-open sports car door;
running anxious and stubborn, you yelled at me
with a little childish cry in your voice:
"A Pa,[2] won't you take me with you? Won't you pay for my
    trip?"
It was the journey of life: and only in a dream therefore
would you dare to discover yourself and ask me for something.
You know very well that that dream is a part of reality;
and it's not a dreamed Ninetto who said those words.
It's so very true that when we speak of it you blush.
Last evening, in Arezzo, in the silence of the night
while the guard closed the gate behind your back
with a chain, and you were at the point of disappearing,
with your sudden and comical smile you said to me . . .
    "Thanks."
"Thanks, Ninne?" It's the first time you said that to me.
And in fact you realized it and corrected yourself without los-
    ing face
(you're a master at that), joking,
"Thanks for the hitch." The trip you wanted,

---

1. Nickname (affectionate) of Ninetto Davoli (below), who was an actor and lover
of Pasolini.
2. Nickname of Pasolini himself.

which I paid for was, I repeat, the journey of life:
it's in that dream of three or four years ago that I decided
what my ambiguous love of liberty was against.
If now you thank me for the passage . . . my God,
while you're in the joint, I'll be afraid of taking
a plane to a faraway place. I'm insatiable about our life
because something unique in the world can never be
    exhausted.

               1969. Translated by Jack Hirschman

THE PRESENCE
to Maria Callas

What was lost was heavenly
and the sick soul holy.
Nothingness was a wind that inexplicably changed
directions but ever and always conscious of its goals.
In the void, which stirred,
inspired from above,
capricious as a stream down below,
what mattered was always a story
that in some manner was begun
and had to continue: yours.
Who was calling me there?
Every morning the tragedy of Being started again
behind shutters first closed then opened as in a Church.
Whether the divine wind blows vainly
or only for those assembled—
the habits, then, those sisters of tragedy—
the sea and the wind heard all our passionate praises,—
your "being is perceiving" ran into tremendous obstacles
to overcome, and every victory was a small one,
and you had to start all over again immediately
like a plant that continually needs water.
But I'm not a brother, Maria;
I fulfill other functions that I don't know;
not that of brotherhood,
at least of that complicity
so very close to obedience and a heroic unawareness
of human beings—your brothers despite everything, not mine.

And you, suspiciously terrified of no longer existing,
know this as well,
and manage to be a mother to yourself.
You allow the little girl in you to be queen,
to open and close the windows as in a ritual
respected by guests, servants and distant spectators.
And yes, but she, she, the little girl—
it's enough for her to feel neglected for a single moment
to feel lost forever;
ah, not because of motionless islands
but because of a fear of not being does the wind stream,
the divine wind
that doesn't heal but rather always makes one sicker;
and you seek to stop her, the one who wants to go back,
but there's not a day, an hour, an instant
in which the desperate effort would cease;
you grasp at anything
and this brings out in people the urge to kiss you.

1970. Translated by Jonathan Richman

LAST THOUGHTS

WHAT IS THIS COUP? I KNOW

I know.

I know the names of those responsible for what has been called a "coup" but what is actually a series of "coups" carried out to ensure the security of power.

I know the names of those responsible for the Milan massacre of December 12, 1969.

I know the names of those responsible for the massacres in Brescia and Bologna in early 1974.

I know the names of the "committee" that manipulated the old fascists into actualizing the "coups," the names of the neofascists who carried out the first massacres and, finally, those of the "unknown" authors of the most recent massacres.

I know the names of those who directed the two different yet opposite phases of the tension strategy: first, the anticommunist phase (Milano 1969), and then the second, antifascist phase (Brescia and Bologna 1974).

I know the names of that group of powerful men who, with the help of the CIA (and then by the "Greek colonels" of the mafia), first created (yet failing miserably) an anticommunist crusade to halt the '68 movement and then, always with the help and inspiration of the CIA, they reconstituted an antifascist virginity so as to stall the disaster of the "referendum."

I know the names of those who, between Holy Masses, gave their directives to young neo-fascists, or, better, neo-nazis (so as to give full weight to the anticommunist tensions). They further assured them and common criminals of their protection, alongside old Generals, whom they kept as a standing reservist organization for an eventual military coup. These privileges are still active today and will most likely last forever for these nameless individuals who will be used to create the next antifascist tension. I know the names of the serious and important ones who are behind the comic characters, like that general of the Forestry Corps who was in Città Ducale[1] (while the forests of Italy burned), or some of the gray and purely organizational characters, like General Miceli.[2]

I know the names of the serious and important people who are behind the tragic young men who chose the suicidal fascist atrocities, and the common criminals, Sicilians or whoever else, who made themselves available, like hired guns or hitmen.

I know all these names and I know all the actions (massacres and attempts on a variety of institutions) of which they've made themselves guilty.

I know. But I do not have the proof. I do not even have the clues.

---

1. A small town near Rieti.
2. A general in the Italian army promoted by NATO, associated with military counterintelligence operations.

I know because I'm an intellectual, a writer who tries to keep track of everything that happens, to know everything that is written, to imagine everything that is unknown or goes unsaid. I'm a person who coordinates even the most remote facts, who pieces together the disorganized and fragmentary bits of a whole, coherent political scene, who re-establishes logic where chance, folly, and mystery seem to reign.

All this is part of my art and of the instinct of my art. I think it quite unlikely that the "plan of my novel" might be wrong; that it may not be in touch with reality, or that my references to events and actual persons are wrong. I also believe that many other intellectuals and writers know what I know as an intellectual and a writer. The reconstruction of the truth regarding what has happened in Italy after 1968 isn't that difficult, after all. That truth—and one feels it with absolute certainty—forms the background of most journalistic and political commentaries and opinions: in other words, not works of imagination or fiction such as my work is by its very nature.

One last example: it's clear that the truth sought to emerge, with all its names, from behind the editorial in the *Corriere della Sera* of November 1, 1974. It's very likely that journalists and politicians even have some proof or, at least, some clues.

But the problem is this: journalists and politicians, even having some proof, and most certainly some clues, don't name names.

Whose responsibility then is it to pronounce these names? Obviously, it's up to whoever has not only the necessary courage but also someone who is not compromised in his relationship with power, and someone who has nothing to lose. That person is an intellectual.

Therefore an intellectual could very well publicly pronounce those names: but he has neither the proof nor the clues.

Power and the world, which, even while not being power, maintains a practical relationship with power, have excluded free intellectuals (by their very nature) from the possibility of having proof and clues.

Someone might object that I, as an intellectual, as an inventor of stories, could enter that explicitly political world (of power or close to power) and, through compromise, participate in the right to share in the proof and clues.

But to such an objection I'd have to answer that it's not possible. It's the very repugnance of entering into such a political world that defines my potential intellectual courage to speak the truth, to name the names.

The intellectual courage of the truth and political practice are presently two irreconcilable realities in Italy. Political practice imposes upon intellectuals—who are profoundly and viscerally despised by the whole of Italian bourgeoisie—a falsely high and noble mandate. In reality, the task of debating moral and ideological problems is servile at best.

If he is given this mandate the intellectual is considered a traitor to his duty. Shouts go up of a "betrayal of the clerics," which is a gratifying alibi for politicians and the servants of power.

But along with power there also exists an opposition to power. In Italy this opposition is so widespread and strong that it represents a power of its own. I'm referring, of course, to the Italian Communist Party.

It's more than certain that at this moment the presence of a great party of opposition such as the Italian Communist Party is the saving grace of Italy and our poor democratic institutions. The Italian Communist Party represents a clean Country within a corrupt Country, an honest Country within a dishonest Country, an intelligent Country within an idiot Country, a wise Country within an ignorant Country, a humanistic Country within a consumerist Country. The Communist Party is a compact unit of leaders, a base, and voters. During these recent years a period of negotiation has opened between the Italian Communist Party, an authentically unified group, and the rest of Italy. The Italian Communist Party has, as a result, become a "Country unto itself," an island. For this very reason, today, as never before, it's able to have a very close relationship with actual power, corrupt, inept, and degraded as this power is. But these are diplomatic relationships, similar to those between nations. In actuality the two realities are incommensurable, understood in their concreteness, in their totality. It's possible to project on this very basis that realistic "compromise" that might in fact save Italy from falling apart at the seams. This "compromise" might be considered to be an "alliance" between two bordering states, or between two states jammed one inside the other.

But all the positive things that I've said about the Italian Communist Party make up its relatively negative aspects as well.

The division of the country into two separate nations, one up to its neck in degradation and degeneration, and the other intact and uncompromised, can't be a good reason for peace and constructivism.

Furthermore, conceived in this way, as I've outlined it, as a nation within a nation, the opposition identifies with *another* power that is nevertheless still and always power. As a result, the politicians that make up this opposition cannot but behave themselves like men of power.

In the specific instance that at this moment so dramatically concerns us, they too have deferred to the intellectual a mandate of their making. So, if the intellectual doesn't meet the expectations of this purely moral and ideological mandate, he is, to everyone's satisfaction, nothing more than a traitor.

And now, why don't even the politicians of the opposition, if they have—and most likely they do—proof or at least clues, name the names of those truly responsible, of the politicians, of the laughable coups, and of the terrifying massacres of the last few years? Simple: they don't name them as a result of the fact that they make a distinction between political truth and political practice, something an intellectual would not do. And so, naturally, they too keep the intellectual in the dark about proof and clues. Given the objective factual situation, they don't even give it a second thought.

The intellectual has to continue to keep to what is imposed on him as his duty, to reiterate his codified mode of intervention.

I know very well that to make a public motion of non-confidence against the entire political class in Italy, at this particular time in history, would be undiplomatic and rather inopportune. But these political categories, and not political truth, are what the impotent intellectual is required to serve, however and whenever.

Very well, for the very reason that I can't name those responsible for the attempted coups and the massacres (and not in place of it), I can't make my weak and idealistic accusation against the entire Italian political class.

Let it be known that I act fully believing in politics. I believe in the "formal" principles of democracy, I believe in the Parliament, and I believe in political parties. Obviously these beliefs are filtered through my own particular communist view.

I'd be ready and eager to recall my motion of non-confidence if some politician would decide to name the names of those responsible for the coups and massacres. But his decision would have to not be opportunistic, i.e, the moment has come, but rather as a way to create the possibility for such a moment. This politician might decide to name the names of those responsible for the coups and the massacres, which he evidently knows as I do. The difference between us is that he cannot but have the proof, or at least some clues.

Most likely—if the U.S.A. will permit—maybe "diplomatically" deciding to concede to another democracy that which American democracy has conceded itself in the case of Nixon—these names will be named. But, even if this happens, the names will be pronounced by men who have shared in their power. It will be a case of those least responsible against those most responsible. And, as in the American case, it doesn't mean that they'll be any better than the others. That would most definitely be a true coup d'état.

1974. Translated by Pasquale Verdicchio

WE'RE ALL IN DANGER

The last interview with Pier Paolo Pasolini

By Furio Colombo

This interview took place on Saturday, November 1, 1975, between four and six in the evening, a few hours before Pasolini's assassination. I want to emphasize that the title as it appears was his, and not of my own making. As a matter of fact, at the end of the conversation which, as in the past, found us on opposite sides of certain points, I asked him if he wanted to give me a title for the interview. He thought about it awhile, said it wasn't important, changed the topic, and then something brought us back to the subject that had emerged time and again in the answers that follow. "Here is the seed, the sense of everything," he said. "You don't even know who, right at this moment, might be thinking of killing you. Use this as a title, if you like: 'Because, we are all in danger.'"

FC: Pasolini, in your articles and in your writings you've given various accounts of what you detest. You've carried out a solitary struggle against so many things: institutions, trends, people, and power. In order to make things easier, I will refer to it all as the "situation," by which you know that I mean everything against which you generally battle. Let me propose one objection. The "situation," with all its evils as you describe it, also contains all that makes Pasolini possible. What I mean is that, even with all your talent and merit, your tools are provided by the "situation": publishing, cinema, organization, even objects. Let's say that yours is a magic thought. One little gesture and everything that you detest disappears. What about you, then, wouldn't you be left all alone and without any of the tools you need? I mean, the means or tools of expression, I mean. . . .

PPP: I understand. But I not only attempt to achieve that magic thought process, I believe in it. Not as a way to mediate with the world, but because I know that by constantly hitting the same nail on the head one can possibly make a whole house fall down. We find a small example of this among the Radical Party, a motley crew that is able to influence the whole country. You know that I don't always agree with them, but I am about to leave right now for their conference. Most of all, it's history that gives us the best example. Contestation has always been an essential act. Saints, hermits, and intellectuals, those few who've made history, are the ones who've said "no," not the courtesans and Cardinals' assistants. In order to be meaningful, contestation must be large, major, and total, "absurd" and not in good sense. It can't merely be on this or that point. Eichmann had a good lot of good sense. What was he lacking then? He didn't say "no" right away, at the beginning, when he was a mere administrator, a bureaucrat. He might have said to some of his friends, "I don't really like Himmler." He might have whispered something, the way it's done in publishing firms, the newspaper office, in sub-government, in the newsrooms. Or he might even have objected to the fact that some train had stopped once a day for the deported to do their business, for bread and water, when two stops might have been more practical and economical. But he never stopped the machine. And so, there are three arguments to make here: what is what you call the "situation," why should we halt it or destroy it, and how?

FC: Well, describe the "situation" then. You know very well that your observations and your language are like the sun shining through the dust. It's a beautiful image, but things are sometimes a little unclear.

PPP: I thank you for the sun image, but expect much less than that. All I want is that you look around and take notice of the tragedy. What is the tragedy? It's that there are no longer any human beings; there are only some strange machines that bump up against each other. And we intellectuals look at old train schedules and say: "Strange, shouldn't these trains run by there? How come they crashed like that? Either the engineer's lost his mind, or he's a criminal. Or, even better, it's all a conspiracy." We're particularly pleased with conspiracies because they relieve us of the weight of having to deal with the truth head on. Wouldn't it be wonderful if, while we're here talking, someone in the basement were making plans to kill us? It's easy, it's simple, and it's the resistance. We might lose a few friends, but then we'll gather our forces and wipe them out. A little for us, a little for them, don't you think? And I know that when they show *Is Paris Burning?* on TV, everyone sits there with tears in their eyes, wishing only that history would repeat itself, but cleanly and beautifully. The effect of time is that it washes thing clean, like the walls of a house in the rain. It's simple, I'm on this side, and you're on the other. Let's not joke about the blood, the pain, the work that people then also paid with, so as to "have a choice." When one keeps one's face flat against that hour, that minute in history, choice is always a tragedy. But, let's admit, it was easier then. With courage and conscience, a normal man can always reject a

Fascist of Salò[1] or a Nazi of the SS, even from his interior life (where the revolution *always* begins). But today it's different. Someone might come walking toward you dressed like a friend, very friendly and polite, but he's a "collaborator" (let's say for a TV station). The reasoning goes that first of all he needs to make a living somehow, and then because it's not like he's hurting anyone. Another one, or others, the groups come toward you aggressively with their ideological blackmail, their admonitions, their sermons, and their anathemas that are also threats. They march with flags and slogans, but what separates them from "power"?

FC: Well, what is power in your opinion? Where is it? How does one cause it to reveal itself?

PPP: Power is an educational system that divides us into subjects and subjected. Nevertheless, it's an educational system that forms us all, from the so-called ruling class all the way down to the poorest of us. That's why everyone wants the same things and everyone acts in the same way. If I have access to an administrative council or a stock market maneuver, that's what I use. Otherwise I use a crowbar. And when I use a crowbar, I'll use whatever means to get what I want. Why do I want it? Because I've been told that it's a virtue to have it. I'm merely exercising my virtue-rights. I'm a murderer but I'm a good person.

---

1. The town where the Fascists set up their government center after the fall of the government in Milan. It was the name Pasolini gave to his final film, perhaps the most scandalously courageous film ever made.

FC: You've been accused of not being able to make political or ideological distinctions. It's said that you've lost the ability of differentiating the sign of the deep difference that there is between fascists and non-fascists, among the new generations for example.

PPP: That's what I was talking about when I mentioned the train schedules before. Have you ever seen those marionettes that make children laugh so much because their body faces one direction while their heads face another? I think Totò[2] was quite adept at such a trick. Well, that's how I see that wonderful troop of intellectuals, sociologists, experts, and journalists with the most noble of intentions. Things happen here, and their heads are turned in the opposite direction. I'm not saying that there is no fascism. What I'm saying is: don't talk to me of the sea while we're in the mountains. This is a different landscape. There's a desire to kill here. And this desire ties us together as sinister brothers of the sinister failure of an entire social system. I too would like it if it were easy to isolate the black sheep. I too see the black sheep. I see quite a lot of them. I see all of them. That's the problem, as I said to Moravia: given the life I lead, I pay a price . . . it's like a descent into hell. But when I come back—if I come back—I've seen other things, more things. I'm not asking you to believe me. I'm saying that you always find yourselves changing the topic so as to avoid facing the truth.

FC: And what's the truth?

---

2. The great Italian comedian who was the star in Pasolini's poetic masterpiece *Sparrows and Hawks*.

PPP: I'm sorry I used that word. What I wanted to say was "evidence." Let me re-order things. First tragedy: a common education, obligatory and wrong, that pushes us all into the same arena of having to have everything at all costs. In this arena we're pushed along like some strange and dark army in which some carry cannons and others carry crowbars. Therefore, the first classical division is to "stay with the weak." But what I say is that, in a certain sense, everyone is weak, because everyone's a victim. And everyone's guilty, because everyone's ready to play the murderous game of possession. We've learned to have, possess, and destroy.

FC: Let me go back to the first question then. You magically abolish everything. But you live from books, and you need intelligent people who read . . . educated consumers of an intellectual product. You are a filmmaker and, as such, you need large venues (you are very successful, and are "consumed" avidly by your public) but also an extensive technical, managerial, and industrial machine that is in the midst of it all. If you remove all of this, with a sort of magical paleo-Catholic and neo-Chinese monasticism, what's left?

PPP: Everything. I am what is left, being alive, being in the world, a place to see, to work and understand. There are hundreds of ways to tell the stories, to listen to languages, to reproduce dialects, to make puppetry. The others are left with much more. They can keep pace with me, cultured like me or ignorant like me. The world becomes bigger, everything's ours and there's no need to use the stock market, the administrative council, or the crowbar to plunder. You see, in the world that we dreamed about (let me repeat myself: reading old train schedules from either a year or 30 years ago), there was the awful landlord in a top hat and dollars pouring out of his pockets, and the emaciated widow and her children who begged for mercy, as in Brecht's beautiful world.

FC: Are you saying that you miss that world?

PPP: No! My nostalgia is for those poor and real people who struggled to defeat the landlord without becoming that landlord. Since they were excluded from everything, they remained uncolonized. I'm afraid of these Black revolutionaries who are the same as their landlords, equally criminal, who want everything at any cost. This gloomy ostentation toward total violence makes it hard to distinguish to which "side" one belongs. Whoever might be taken to an emergency ward close to death is probably more interested in what the doctors have to tell him about his chances of living than what the police might have to say about the mechanism of the crime. Be assured that I'm neither condemning intentions nor am I interested in the chain of cause and effect: them first, him first, or who's the primary guilty party. I think we've defined what you called the "situation." It's like it rains in the city and the gutters are backed up. The water rises, but the water's innocent, it's rainwater. It has neither the fury of sea nor the rage of river current. But, for some reason, it rises instead of falling. It's the same water of so many adolescent poems and of the cutesy songs like "Singing in the Rain." But it rises and it drowns you. If that's where we are, I say let's not waste time placing nametags here and there. Let's see then how we can unplug this tub before we all drown.

FC: And to get there you would want everyone to be ignorant and happy little unschooled shepherds?

PPP: Put in those terms it would be absurd. But the educational system as it is can't but produce desperate gladiators. The masses are growing, as is desperation and rage. Let's say that I've flung a *boutade* (but I don't think so), what else can you come up with? Of course I lament a pure revolution led by oppressed peoples whose only goal is to free themselves and run their own lives. Of course I try to imagine that such a moment might still be possible in Italian and world history. The best of what I imagine might even inspire one of my future poems. But not what I know and what I see. I want to say it plainly and clearly: I go down into hell and I see things that don't disturb the peace of others. But be careful. Hell is rising toward the rest of you. It's true that it dreams its own uniform and its own justification (sometimes). But it's also true that its desire, its need to hit back, to assault, to kill, is strong and wide-ranging. The private and risky experience of those who've touched "the violent life" will not be available for long. Don't be fooled. And you are, along with the educational system, television, the pacifying newspapers, the great keepers of this horrendous order founded on the concept of possession and the idea of destruction. Luckily, you seem to be happy when you can tag a murder with its own beautiful description. This to me is just another one of mass culture's operations. Since we can't prevent certain things from happening, we find peace in constructing shelves on which to keep them.

FC: But to abolish also means to create, unless you too are a destroyer. What happens to the books, for example? I certainly don't want to be one of those people who's anguished by the loss of culture more than for people. But these people saved in your vision of a different world can no longer be primitive (an accusation often leveled at you), and if we don't want to repress "more advanced" . . . .

PPP: Which makes me cringe.

FC: If we don't want to fall back on commonplaces, there must be some sort of clue. For example, in science fiction, as in Nazism, book burning is always the first step in the massacres. Once you've shut down the schools and abolished television, how do you animate your world?

PPP: I think I already covered this with Moravia. Closing or abolishing in my language means "to change." But change in a drastic and desperate manner, such as the situation dictates. What really prevents a real dialogue with Moravia, but more so with Firpo,[3] for example, is that somehow we're not seeing the same scene, we don't know the same people, and that we don't hear the same voices. For you and them, things happen when it's news, beautifully written, formatted, cut, and titled. But what's underneath it all? What's missing is a surgeon who has the courage to examine the tissue and declare: gentlemen, this is cancer, and it's not benign. What is cancer? It's something that changes all the cells, which causes them to grow in a haphazard manner, outside of any previous logic. Is a cancer patient who dreams about the same healthy body he had before nostalgic, even if before he was stupid and unlucky? Before the cancer, I mean. First of all one

---

3. Attilio Firpo, d. 1945, a poet and activist in the Resistance. He was 29 when he was killed by the Fascists.

would have to make quite an effort to re-establish the same image. I listen to all the politicians and their little formulas, and it drives me insane. They don't seem to know what country they're talking about; they're as distant as the Moon. And the same goes for the writers, sociologists, and experts of all sorts.

FC: Why do you think that some things are so evident for you?

PPP: I don't want to talk about myself anymore. Maybe I've said too much already. Everyone knows that I pay for my experiences in person. But there are also my books and my films. Maybe I'm wrong, but I'll keep on saying that we're all in danger.

FC: Pasolini, if that's how you see life—I don't know if you'll accept this question— how do you hope to avoid the risk and danger involved?

It's late, Pasolini hasn't turned on any lights, and it's become hard to take notes. We look over what I've written. Then he asks me to leave the questions with him.

PPP: There are some statements that seem a little too absolute. Let me think about it, let me look them over. And give me the time to come up with a concluding remark. I have something in mind for your question. I find it easier to write than to talk. I'll give you the notes that I'll add tomorrow morning.

The next day, Sunday, Pasolini's body was in the morgue of the Rome police station.

1975. Translated by Pasquale Verdicchio

Susanna Bonetti was born in Alfonsine, near Ravenna, Italy, and came to the United States in 1984. She works at the Erik Erikson Library at the San Francisco Center for Psychoanalysis.

Veruska Cantelli is a writer and translator who has also collaborated on several film and documentary projects. Originally from Rome, she lives in New York City, where she is completing her Ph.D. in Comparative Literature at the City University of New York. She teaches Comparative Literature at Queens College of CUNY, is a member of the Human Kinetics Movement Arts, and is currently co-writing a feature screenplay titled *Notown*.

Giada Diano was born in Reggio Calabria and earned a degree in foreign languages and literature at Messina University and a Ph.D in English and Anglo-American studies at Catania University. Author of *Io sono come Omero*, a biography of the poet Lawrence Ferlinghetti, she has also worked as a translator and curator. She is the founder of the Angoli Corsari Cultural Association, which promotes cultural events in the south of Italy.

Lucia Gazzino was born in Udine (Friuli, Italy) in 1959 and has been a poet since she was a teenager. A teacher of creative writing, she translates history and poetry, and writes both in Italian and in Friulian (her mother tongue). Her poems have appeared in various anthologies of Italian poetry, and have been translated into German and English. Her books include *Fiori di Papiro*, *La cjase des Cjartis*, and *Alter Mundus*. Her poetic DVD is called *Viaggiatori senza Valigia*. In 2005,

Marimbo Press published *The New Youth*, her translation of twenty Friulian poems by Pier Paolo Pasolini.

Renowned poet Jack Hirschman was the fourth poet laureate of San Francisco and is now Poet-in-Residence with the Friends of the San Francisco Public Library. His City Lights volumes include *Lyripol, Front Lines*, and *All That's Left*. He also edited the seminal *Artaud Anthology* for City Lights in 1965. His major work is *The Arcanes*, published in 2006 by Multimedia Edizioni of Salerno.

Norman MacAfee selected and translated with Luciano Martinengo *Poems*, the first English-language edition of Pasolini's poetry. MacAfee's *One Class: Selected Poems* was published by Harbor Mountain in 2008. With Lee Fahnestock, he co-translated Victor Hugo's *Les Misérables* and two volumes of the letters of Jean-Paul Sartre, edited by Simone de Beauvoir. The Massachusetts International Festival of the Arts will premiere MacAfee's opera *The Death of the Forest* in 2013.

Jonathan Richman sings and plays guitar for a living. He also does stone and brickwork and now translations from Italian into American. He thanks Jacobo Menci of Rome for his enormous help, especially in the understanding of Pasolini's references to events and places specifically Roman.

Flavio Rizzo is a writer and filmmaker. After receiving an Italian Laurea in Cinema Studies at the University of Rome, he directed a documentary about Pier Paolo Pasolini titled *Not to Money, Nor to Love, Neither to the Sky*, which went on to receive the Cinema Avvenire award at the 54th Venice Film Festival. He recently directed the documentary *Cuidad de Los Niños* about an orphanage in Cochabamba, Bolivia trapped in the Coca Wars. He is now working on a feature length screenplay titled *Notown*, and a documentary that profiles writer Ayi Kwei Armah through a lyrical journey across West Africa. He lives in New York and teaches Comparative Literature at Queens College of CUNY.

Pasquale Verdicchio teaches in the Department of Literature at UC San Diego. In addition to essays on Italian and Italian-American culture, he has translated the work of Pasolini, Zanzotto, Caproni, Merini, and Gramsci among others. His latest book of poetry is *This Nothing's Place*.